RED& WHITE QUILTING

An Iconic Tradition in 40 Blocks

LINDA PUMPHREY

Fons&Porter

![fw logo] a content + ecommerce company

www.fwcommunity.com

21 20 19 18 17   5 4 3 2 1

Distributed in Canada by Fraser Direct
100 Armstrong Avenue
Georgetown, ON, Canada L7G 5S4
TEL: (905) 877-4411

Distributed in the U.K. and Europe by
F&W MEDIA INTERNATIONAL
Pynes Hill Court, Pynes Hill, Rydon Lane
Exeter, EX2 5AZ, United Kingdom
TEL: (+44) 1392 797680
E-MAIL: enquiries@fwmedia.com

SRN: R2718

ISBN 13: 978-1-4402-4744-6

EDITORIAL DIRECTOR: Kerry Bogert
EDITOR: Jodi Butler
TECHNICAL EDITOR: Debra Fehr Greenway
ART DIRECTOR: Ashlee Wadeson
COVER AND INTERIOR DESIGNER: Julia Boyles
ILLUSTRATOR: April Wickett
PHOTOGRAPHER: Dean Schoeppner
COVER PHOTOGRAPHER: George Boe

CONTENTS

FOREWORD

DEBORAH ROBERTS, noted quilt and textile historian, quilt appraiser certified by AQS, and Founder, World of Quilts Travel

We live in a world that is infatuated with color, and perhaps no color has influenced the world of quiltmaking more than Turkey red. Since the early nineteenth century, the combination of Turkey red cotton and white fabric has been a classic color scheme. Aside from the simple and graphic appeal of the contrast, quilters loved Turkey red because it was colorfast and did not fade.

In terms of fabric, Turkey red is exclusively attributed to bright, clear, cherry-red cotton. However, this color is the result of a unique dying process, which began in India and moved west to the region around Turkey and Greece known as the Levant. It was a costly and complex method involving up to seventeen steps, with many steps repeated multiple times. Until the process was refined, it took up to twenty-five days to produce this brilliant red color on cotton.

The brightly-dyed colorfast cottons from the East were a far cry from the drab, faded palette of seventeenth century Europe, and the demand for a pure, bright cloth that would not fade was overwhelming. European dyers sought to duplicate the red-colored cloth, but the dye recipe was a closely protected secret. So, European manufacturers sent spies to the Levant to learn the tedious dyeing process. This early industrial espionage was initially unsuccessful and Europe continued to import red yarn from Turkey and red fabric from India throughout the first half of the eighteenth century.

In 1747, a French manufacturer in Rouen, France, enticed dyers from Greece to teach him the elusive process. Once the recipe was revealed, Europeans began to successfully create the brilliant color using the chemical alizarin, which was taken from the root of a madder plant.

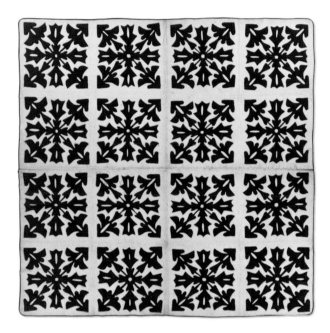

Lobster
1890–1910
Maker Unknown
7.5" × 7.5½"
(190.5 cm × 192 cm)

Oak Reel
1850–1870
Maker Unknown
91½" × 92"
(232.5 cm × 233.5 cm)

Basket
1840–1860
Maker Unknown
80" × 100" (203 cm × 254 cm)

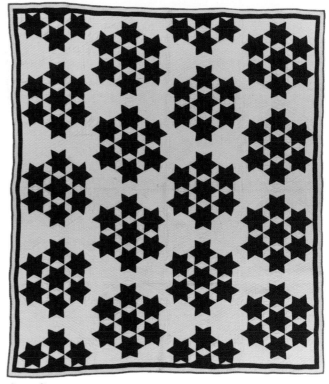

Seven Sisters
1850–1870
Maker Unknown
66½" × 80" (169 cm × 203 cm)

They also used the chemical alum to fix the dye, along with multiple and repeated processes of soaking the yarns in lye, animal fat, urine, dung, and other ingredients.

Early on, to obtain a uniformly colored fabric, European manufacturers first dyed cotton yarn and wove it into red cloth. By 1765, woven Turkey red cotton cloth production was in full-swing in France, England, Scotland, and Holland as dyers throughout the region continued to refine the process. Around the turn of the nineteenth century, Europeans successfully managed to develop a method of dyeing pre-woven cotton yard goods the intense red.

Initially, printing onto Turkey red fabric was virtually impossible, as the oils used in the process of dyeing would not allow additional dyes to penetrate the surface of the cloth. In 1810, after multiple attempts by printers throughout the region, Daniel Kochelin, a textile printer from Mulhouse, France, developed a method to discharge

print on Turkey red. He bleached out the red color in a certain motif and replaced the bleached color with black or blue and eventually yellow. By 1815, multiple color prints on Turkey red fabric were available.

Turkey red prints became a hit throughout the European region and were seen in garments as well as household linens. Manufacturers in England, France, and Scotland began to export both solid and printed Turkey red fabric to the United States, Africa, and the Middle East. England and Scotland also exported the fabric to India. By the early 1830s, exports of the cloth to the United States were almost nonstop as boatloads of solid and printed Turkey red fabrics arrived on American shores where they were quickly consumed. Quiltmakers fell in love with the vivid and colorfast quality, paying a premium for the bright red fabrics.

The earliest use of Turkey red in American quilts began around 1830 as quilters used small-scale floral and

geometric prints, primarily in appliquéd pieces. By 1840, white and red fabric quilts became popular and the trend lasted for twenty years. In 1868, a synthetic version of the alizarin dye was invented, which lowered the price of the fabric and ushered in a second craze of Turkey red and white quiltmaking. Respective to quilters in their own regions, European textile manufacturers also catered specifically to the quilting market by printing whole cloth panels and cheater-cloth patchwork fabric motifs in the last half of the nineteenth century.

In the early twentieth century, an even less costly synthetic Turkey red dye was available around the same time that the color's use in quilts expanded to include embroidery work comprised of subjects and signatures with red thread on white fabric. Used in various motifs and techniques, Turkey red and white remained a popular color combination among quiltmakers throughout the early twentieth century.

PREFACE

CAROLYN DUCEY, PhD, Curator of Collections, International Quilt Study Center & Museum, Quilt House, University of Nebraska–Lincoln

Brilliant red dyed fabrics became part of the European and North American quilt vocabulary in the mid-nineteenth century. The color, a result of a technically complex process called "Turkey red" was first encountered by European textile manufacturers in Central Asia in the mid-seventeenth century. Entranced by its beauty, they became determined to learn the complex dye process. Manufacturers sent spies to Turkey and later to other European cities to uncover the coveted methods, and they imported workers to set up and operate dyehouses specializing in the process. Strong centers of Turkey red dyeing developed in France, Holland, and Scotland.

Papercut Appliqué
1852
Maker: Helen E. Loury
Size: 82½" × 98¼"
(209.5 cm × 249.5 cm)

THE COLOR RED REMAINS A PERENNIAL FAVORITE.

As the nineteenth century dawned, technological advances in cotton production and printing made it easier and quicker to produce Turkey red fabrics, which made them more available and affordable. They were especially loved because of their colorfast, durable quality.

The influx of Turkey red printed cottons in the United States greatly influenced quilt styles. Pennsylvanian quiltmakers first used Turkey red printed fabrics in an appliqué style that became overwhelmingly popular between 1840 and 1860. Stylized floral designs were repeated in block formats, framed by swaying floral borders. In the last years of the nineteenth century, red fabric, now produced with a variety of synthetic dyes, became a popular color trend again, seen in two-color pieced quilts and in twentieth-century embroidered redwork quilts. The color red remains a perennial favorite.

Red & White Quilting illustrates traditional red and white quilts alongside new interpretations by designer and maker Linda Pumphrey. With her inventive perspective and eye for innovation, Pumphrey creates dynamic contemporary quilts with patterns that are both familiar and different to us. They are fresh interpretations in unique combinations and forms that show how we retain a love for red today.

For the second time in as many years, Pumphrey once again has produced a book that offers a new approach to historic designs while also benefiting the International Quilt Study Center & Museum. Proceeds from the sale of this book and her first, *Mountain Mist Historical Quilts*, will significantly contribute to the preservation of the museum's collections. We are incredibly fortunate to have such wonderful continuing support.

INTRODUCTION

The vibrant contrast of red and white quilts has appealed to quilters for three centuries and has been a staple since the mid-nineteenth century. Just looking at various red and white quilts, it is easy to see why. Two-color quilts are graphic and stunning. In a two-color quilt, the pattern creates visual impact while the quilting design shows the background story of the quilt. The contrast between red and white is rich in meaning and historical significance.

Red, more than any other color on the color wheel, has many implications and evokes intense feelings, both good and bad.

Red is associated with passion, desire, and love. In the Eastern world, red represents good luck, and it is traditional for brides to wear a red wedding dress. Worldwide, red roses are the most common gift of love.

Red can also mean danger. It is a highly visual color and is often used to indicate warnings. For this reason, emergency lights on ambulances, fire trucks, and police cars are red. Throughout the world, red is the color for stop signs and stop lights.

Red is also the most popular color used in flags and often symbolizes strength and pride. The color red can imply power, wealth, and nobility. In seventeenth-century France, King Louis XIV loved to flaunt his legs and frequently wore red stockings or shoes with red heels. Other nobles from surrounding European countries copied the French court fashion and the red heels. Red heels on shoes are a fashion statement which still exists today.

In contrast, the color white has almost the opposite meanings of red. White is a positive color associated with innocence, completeness, and perfection. It is the color of peace, with a white dove being the

Crosses
1830–1850
Maker Unknown
36" x 37"
(91.5 cm x 94 cm)

symbol for this meaning. A white flag means surrender. White in the Western world depicts purity, making it the traditional color of bridal gowns in Western culture.

White is often used to represent openness, truth, and simplicity. It is associated with religious figures, such as angels who are either depicted wearing white or surrounded by a white light.

While white is not a color that stimulates intense feelings or emotions, it is a color that allows our minds to be like a blank page. With the impact of the color red and the

passive nature of the color white, it is no wonder that these two colors are popular pairings for quilts and have stood the test of time.

For inspiration for this book, we have drawn from the extensive red and white quilt collection at the International Quilt Study Center & Museum, University of Nebraska-Lincoln. The museum has over eighty red and white quilts spanning several centuries with the oldest, Crosses, dating back to 1830s. These wonderfully graphic quilts include both appliqué and pieced designs that range from simplistic to very involved.

Carpenter's Square
1880–1910
Maker Unknown
74" (188 cm)

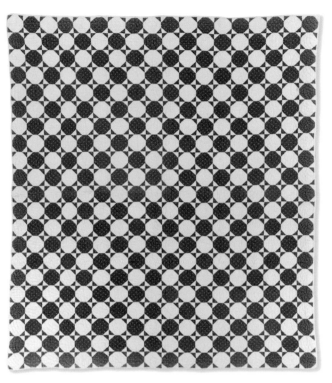

Rob Peter to Pay Paul
1890–1910
Maker Unknown
66" × 75" (167.5 cm × 190.5 cm)

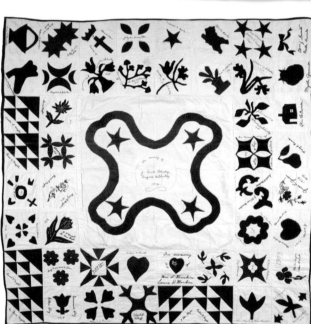

Album
1908–1914
Maker Unknown
63½" × 65½" (161.5 cm × 166.5 cm)

There are block patterns that easily lend themselves to a two-color quilt. Some traditional favorites include Snowball, Rob Peter to Pay Paul, Goose in the Pond, Carpenter's Square, Album, and Oak Reel. While pieced work is the most common technique seen in two-color quilts, some of the quilts used for inspiration for this book contain wonderful appliqué patterns.

This book presents forty quilt blocks and fourteen projects inspired by the museum's quilts. Many of the designs have been simplified or the scale changed to enhance the graphic nature of the blocks, which are incorporated into the featured quilts and smaller projects. If your favorite block isn't highlighted in a specific project, do not worry. Many of the same-size blocks are interchangeable, so you can often substitute the blocks you like for the ones shown in

the patterns. Each featured project also includes alternative designs using different blocks. There are many options to choose from.

Happy quilting!

— Linda

CHAPTER 1

TOOLS & TECHNIQUES

Having the right tools on hand and a basic guide to quilting techniques and tips will help make the process of quilting easier and more enjoyable. There are several methods and rules that guide a quilter, and sometimes there is more than one way to accomplish the same result. The following are the tips that I have found to be the most helpful.

THERE IS MORE THAN ONE WAY TO ACCOMPLISH THE SAME RESULT.

TOOLS OF THE TRADE

Here are my go-to supplies for creating the projects in this book:

- ▶ Fusible lightweight interfacing
- ▶ Spray fabric sizing
- ▶ Coordinating threads for piecing and appliquéing (#40 or #50 is desirable for machine piecing and raw-edge machine appliqué)
- ▶ Contrasting thread for basting
- ▶ Sewing machine needles
- ▶ Fabric glue
- ▶ Safety pins
- ▶ Ball-end straight pins
- ▶ Binder clips
- ▶ Rotary cutter and mat
- ▶ Fabric die cutter and dies (see Die Cutting)
- ▶ Quilting rulers: 6½" × 24" (16.5 cm × 61 cm) and 12½" (31.5 cm) square
- ▶ Fabric scissors
- ▶ Erasable fabric pencil
- ▶ Sewing machine with ¼" (6 mm) quilting foot
- ▶ Steam iron and ironing board
- ▶ Light box

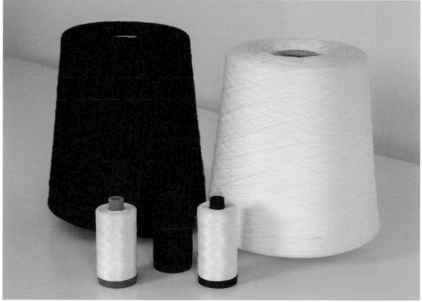

CHOOSING FABRIC

When making a two-color quilt, choosing fabric becomes easy. However, each of the projects in this book can be made using a variety of fabrics and colors. With so many colors and patterns to choose from these days, it can be hard to decide which fabrics to use. Here are some things to keep in mind whether you choose to use red and white or venture into more than two colors.

BUY THE BEST QUALITY FABRIC YOUR BUDGET WILL ALLOW. Lesser quality fabrics will have a lower thread count, which means the fabric may stretch more easily.

Stretching in turn can be a problem when you are cutting and sewing shapes together. Colors are normally printed on a lower thread-count fabric, so look for fabric that has at least a 60 square thread count on both the warp and weft.

CONSIDER THE DESIGN. In a two-color quilt, such as red and white, using white as the background fabric will accentuate the red design elements. If red is used as the background or dominant color, then the white design elements stand out.

IF CHOOSING MORE THAN TWO COLORS, PICK A PALETTE THAT PLEASES YOU. Each color has a role to play. The main fabric will be the dominant color in the quilt. Sometimes this is the background fabric. The background fabric sets the stage for the design elements in the quilt. If the background is too busy or overwhelming, the design may get lost. Secondary colors support the main color. You can have more than one secondary color. Accent colors add a small pop of interest.

CHOOSE FABRICS WITH DIFFERENT TONES. Using a combination of light, medium, and dark tones will give a quilt extra personality. A small amount of dark fabric will give the design depth.

MAKE SURE NEUTRAL COLORS WORK TOGETHER. When working with neutrals, make sure the whites are the same tone. Pairing a white with a print that has an off-white background may not look right.

PAY ATTENTION TO PRINTS. When you are working with prints, consider the scale of the design. For smaller pieces, such as the shapes in the Mirror Image block, a large print may get lost. In a pattern with large pieces, a small print may read as a solid when the quilt top is done.

TO PREWASH OR NOT TO PREWASH FABRIC

Because the sizing in fabric can help with the cutting and sewing process of making a quilt, some quiltmakers choose not to prewash their fabrics. However, vibrant colors, such as reds and purples, tend to bleed more than

others when washed. If you do not prewash your fabric and bleeding occurs, it can damage the finished quilt.

When Should You Prewash Fabric?

1. If you're concerned about colors bleeding, definitely prewash your fabric. In a two-color quilt, especially a red and white combination, it is wise to be cautious and prewash your fabric. Or at least test your fabric for color fastness. To test your fabric, cut a small colored square, about 6" (15 cm), and rub it against an all-white fabric square of about the same size. Do both a dry test and a wet test to determine if any color transfers:

▸ Perform a dry test to make sure that the fabric color does not crock (transfer color) when rubbing the darker fabric against the lighter fabric. Rub the fabrics together about ten times. If you see any color transfer, then you will need to prewash your fabric.

▸ Perform a wet test to make sure the fabric color does not bleed. Wet both the light and dark fabric squares and set them against each other for about fifteen minutes. Again, if you see

any color transfer, it is advisable to prewash your fabric.

2. If you are concerned about shrinkage of the fabric, you should prewash fabric (for tips, see Preparing Fabric for Prewashing).

NOTE: *All 100 percent cotton fabrics shrink, some more than others.*

Preparing Fabric for Prewashing

Fabric can fray giving you stringy edges and sometimes fabric waste when washing, so it is helpful to prepare fabric before washing it. You can:

▸ Cut the edges with a pinking rotary blade or scissors

▸ Sew the raw edges with an open zig-zag stitch

▸ Serge the raw edges of the fabric prior to washing

If you end up prewashing your fabric, you may want to add sizing or starch when you iron the fabric or before you cut it. Sizing will prevent the fabric from stretching during the cutting and sewing process.

MAKING BLOCKS

Three factors go into making those perfect points and corners match: accurate cutting, consistent ¼" (6 mm) seams, and precise pressing of the seams. If you master all three, you will find that points and corners fall into place like a dream. If you only mind the first two, your quilt can go astray at the ironing board. It's important to note that pressing and ironing are different (see Pressing for details).

DIE CUTTING

Using a die cutter can make the cutting part of quilting safer, faster, and more accurate. My favorite cutter is GO! from AccuQuilt. But other brands are also available and have shapes that are just as useful as those in the GO! Library, so comparable shapes can be substituted in their place.

Die cutting shapes allows you to get to the sewing machine faster. For example, for the Courthouse Steps block and projects where clean precise strips are a must, cutting the strips with dies can make all the difference. In addition to saving time, die cutting also ensures that shapes are the same size, which makes them easier to appliqué and adds to the overall beauty of the finished quilt. If you have an embroidery sewing machine, you can even digitize and embroider the shapes in place.

For pieced quilts, die cutting has advantages, too. Accuracy is a must for matching corners and points. In addition, dog-ears can be pretrimmed. Flying geese and half-square triangles, for example, are easier to sew with the pointed edge already trimmed.

Die Cutting: Easy as 1, 2, 3

Follow these steps for more accurate cutting.

1. Place the fabric on the foam side of the die, covering only the shape you are cutting—not the entire die board. Place the cutting mat on top of the fabric to secure it in place. (This is the die/fabric/mat sandwich.)

2. Place the die against the roller. Roll the die/fabric/mat sandwich through the rollers.

HELPFUL HINTS
Making the Best Cuts Possible

- For appliqué shapes, pre-fuse fabric following the manufacturer's directions before cutting.

- Having the fabric faceup on the die will cut the shape as you see it; having the fabric facedown will cut a mirror image.

- Cut only 3 to 4 layers at a time when cutting pre-fused fabric (the fusible layers count as half a layer of fabric).

- For pieced shapes and strips, you can cut up to 6 layers at a time.

- For thicker, lofty fabric such as wool or felt, start by cutting up to 2 to 3 layers at a time.

- For accuracy, cut your piecing shapes on the lengthwise grain.

3. Slide the mat off to remove the perfectly cut shapes. Sliding the mat off keeps the shapes from sticking to its surface. Repeat for the remaining shapes.

PRESSING

Pressing is the motion of lowering and lifting the iron from the fabric surface. Ironing is the back-and-forth motion of the iron on the fabric. While ironing can pull and distort shapes, pressing allows you to turn seam allowances open or lay them to one side without distorting or stretching the fabric.

I'm sure you've heard all the "quilt-pressing rules," such as "always press toward the dark side" or "always press the seams open." When my mom, sister, and I quilt together, the pressing of the quilt top can create controversy. My mom and sister prefer to press seams to the side, while I like to press seams open. Whatever your preference, here are some tips to assure the best-pressed seams:

1. After sewing the seams, always press them with the right sides together to set the stitches into the fabric. (Remember to press, not iron.)

2. Starting with the darker fabric on top, open up the dark fabric piece and press along the seam line. If you prefer to open all the seams, press from the wrong side and gently press the seams open along the seam line.

3. To use steam or not to use steam is another controversial topic. Some quilters love steam, while others never use it. In my experience, it is best to use a dry iron. However, steam might be needed to smooth out seams with lots of points. Instead of steam, you can use a shot of mist from a spray bottle to aid in making sure the seam lies flat.

4. For small shapes, you can finger press the back of your fingernail across the inside of the seam. If

you finger press small shapes, you will still want to press them with an iron to ensure a smooth seam.

5. If a seam is pressed the wrong way, press the shape back to the way it was sewn. Set the seam from the wrong side again, let it cool, and start over.

6. Press a bias seam with your iron at a 45-degree angle and press along the straight-of-grain of the fabric. This works well on shapes such as flying geese and half-square triangles.

PIECING BLOCKS

As you start a quilt, it is helpful to make a complete block to use as reference for the blocks that follow. This way, you can see if you understand the instructions. Accurate piecing is one of the three most important steps in quiltmaking. (Cutting accurately and pressing are the other two.)

When piecing by machine, set the stitch length at 12 stitches per inch (2.5 cm) and use an exact ¼" (6 mm) seam allowance. If your sewing machine has a stitch-length dial, set it at 2 to 2.5. Many sewing machine brands provide a quilting foot to help with sewing an accurate ¼" (6 mm) seam allowance. This sewing foot is well worth the investment. Test your seam accuracy before starting to quilt. When machine piecing shapes together, back stitching isn't necessary. If you're handpiecing, use a small running stitch along the traced lines of each piece. Always begin and end with a small backstitch. Trim and press seams as they are completed.

APPLIQUÉING BLOCKS

Prevent Shadowing

Shadowing can occur when appliquéing a lighter fabric on top of a darker fabric. Lining your appliqué shape with a very lightweight fusible interfacing is a great way to prevent shadowing. When using the needle-turn method, cut the fusible interfacing the size of the template. Cut fabric ¼" (6 mm) larger than the template to allow for the turned-under seam allowance.

Raw Edge Finished Edge

Apply paper-backed fusible web to the wrong side of the fabric according to the manufacturer's directions. Cut strips of "pre-fused" fabric following the pattern directions. You can then pin-baste or glue-baste the

Finding the Center of a Block

To locate the center of the block, gently fold the fabric horizontally, vertically, and diagonally in both directions and crease lightly. Be careful not to stretch the block when folding on the bias (stretch) of the fabric.

strips onto the block. Iron into place. Now you are ready to appliqué using your favorite appliqué stitch.

NOTE: *All strips are cut on the straight-of-grain for the designs in this book.*

Fold Edge Finish

Determine the finished width you want for the stem or curved lines. A basic rule to follow is to cut the strips double the finished width and add ½" (1.3 cm). For example, for a finished ⅜" (1 cm) bias strip, the cut width would be ¾" (2 cm) plus ½" (1.3 cm), or 1¼" (3.3 cm). The extra ½" (1.3 cm) is your ¼" (6 mm) seam allowance on each side. Fold the strip in half with wrong sides together and then sew a ¼" (6 mm) seam along the raw edges. Press the strip to lie flat and then press the strip so the seam is close to one edge along the back of the strip. Glue-baste the strip to the block. Now you can appliqué using your favorite stitch.

SEWING Y-SEAMS

Sewing Y-seams can be challenging. But by following the steps and tips outlined here, you will have them mastered in no time:

1. Mark a dot ¼" (6 mm) in from the point of each side to indicate where to start sewing (FIGURE 1).

2. Sew one side of the seam from the edge to the edge of the dot. Then sew the second seam from the edge to the dot. Take care not to sew past your first seam (FIGURE 2).

3. Press the seams open.

Dots on wrong side

FIGURE 1

Begin

FIGURE 2

3 Tips for Perfecting Y-Seams

- Sew accurate ¼" (6 mm) seams.

- Start and stop exactly at the marked points. You do not want to oversew the corner.

- Sew from the center to the edge. A backstitch at the beginning and end of each seam is helpful to keep the seams from coming apart at the intersections.

CHOOSING THE RIGHT BATTING

The defining characteristic of a quilt is the layer of batting between two layers of cloth that is held in place by stitches. Batting is a soft bulky assembly of fibers, usually carded or opened, that gives quilts their warmth, definition, and resilience. Ideally, the batting you use should complement how you intend to quilt your quilt, the finished look you want, and how you plan to use the quilt. There isn't a universal batting that is perfect for all quilts. But picking the correct batting can be easy if you start with these basic questions:

1. How will the quilt be used? For example, batting for a bed quilt needs drape and should have a "cuddle factor," while a wall quilt needs batting that can hang straight. Is this going to be a baby quilt that will be washed repeatedly or a wall hanging that will rarely get cleaned?

2. How will the project be quilted? Some battings are more suitable for handquilting, while others are better for machine quilting.

3. What quilting-stitch intervals or designs will be used? Do you plan on doing minimal quilting or using a tight pattern that has a lot of quilting?

4. What overall look do you want for the quilting?

Batting Qualities

DRAPABILITY: The thickness and density of the batting will determine the drape as well as the softness and cuddle factor of the finished quilt.

LOFT: The thickness of the batting. A thinner batting will usually give a quilt an old-fashioned appearance and will allow the quilting stitches to lie closer to the surface. A thicker batting will give more relief to the quilting design.

✚ HELPFUL HINT
Clipping Threads

Trimming loose threads is vital. If your seams have raveled, clip the threads. A neat back side of the quilt top takes time and care but is a necessary step.

RESILIENCY: This term describes the ability of the batting to regain its original loft when compressed. Polyester and polyester blends regain their loft fairly quickly and resist creasing or showing fold lines. Natural fibers, such as wool or cotton, have less to little resiliency.

COMFORT FACTOR: Cotton battings breath, making them cooler in the summer and warmer in the winter. Polyester battings are usually hotter to sleep under as they trap the air. Wool batting offers warmth without weight.

WASHABILITY AND SHRINKAGE: Polyester battings and most washable wools do not shrink. Some cotton, cotton blends, and wool can shrink up to 3 to 5%, which gives the finished quilts an old-fashioned appearance. Refer to the manufacturer's packaging, as not all cotton battings shrink at the same rate. Shrinkage can also be controlled by the amount of quilting and whether or not you prewash the fabric.

MACHINE DIRECTION: The machine- or lengthwise-direction of fabric (the warp) is stable and doesn't have much stretch, while the cross-machine or cross-width direction (the weft) has the most give or stretch.

BONDED: Fibers are held together with a spray-on acrylic finish or with a heat process that creates a bond, hence the name. Fibers can also be held together mechanically. For example, in needlepunched batting, the fibers are held together by interweaving them using a bed of needles.

SCRIM: Similar to a lightweight interfacing, scrim is an internal layer that offers extra stability to batting. The fibers are usually needlepunched through.

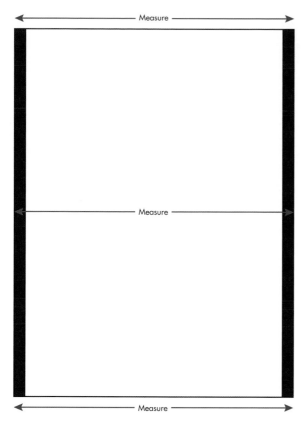

FIGURE 1

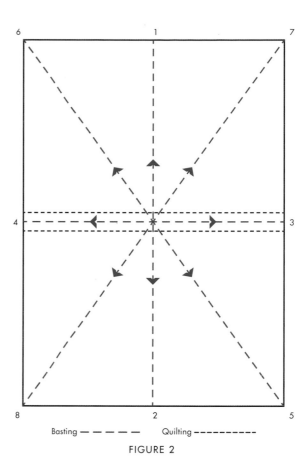

Basting — — — — — Quilting ----------

FIGURE 2

MEASURING BORDERS

You have cut, pressed, and sewn accurately, but your quilt top measurements do not match the pattern and the border measurements are not working. Do not panic! Follow these steps to adjust the border measurements (refer to FIGURE 1).

1. Measure across the length of the quilt in at least three places. For example, measure in the middle of the quilt as well as about one-fourth to one-third in from each side.

2. Average the results: Add, then divide the total by 3. Cut the borders to that length.

3. Sew the border to the quilt top. Press the seams toward the borders.

4. Repeat for the opposite direction.

LAYERING YOUR QUILT TOP

1. Cut the batting and backing at least 4–8" (10–20.5 cm) wider than the quilt top.

NOTE: *The backing will need to be 8" (20.5 cm) wider than the quilt top for longarm quilting.*

2. Press the quilt top and backing so they will lay flat and smooth. Press the backing seams open for less bulk. Be sure to cut off the selvedges if your backing has a seam close to them.

3. If you choose to mark the quilt with a design, draw the design with a removable fabric marker (test on scraps first) before layering the quilt.

NOTE: *If you are going to long arm the quilt, you can skip the following basting steps.*

4. Lay the backing wrong-side up on a flat surface. Tape or pin the backing so it is taut, but not stretched.

5. Center the batting on the backing and gently smooth out the wrinkles.

6. Place the quilt top right-side up on the batting and tape or pin to a flat surface so the top is smooth and taut.

7. Thread-baste or pin-baste the quilt by using large running stitches or quilters' safety pins. Follow the lines on the quilt top (FIGURE 2).

8. Baste additional lines every 3–5" (7.5–12.5 cm) to secure the layers. Pins are recommended when machine quilting.

FRENCH-FOLD BINDING

Binding is the final step for your quilt, providing the finishing touch. Sometimes you want the binding fabric to contrast with the borders. Other times, you may prefer to have the binding blend with the border and use the same fabric for both. Strips for binding may be cut either on the straight-of-grain or on the bias. Bias binding is necessary when working with curved or scalloped edges.

For most quilts, it works to cut the strips on the straight-of-grain. In this book, we used a 2¼" (5.5 cm) wide binding. If you prefer a wider binding, use a 2½" (6.5 cm) strip instead.

NOTE: *You may need slightly more fabric for cutting on the bias.*

Getting Started

1. Measure each side of your quilt, adding about 18" (45.5 cm) to allow for mitered corners and finishing the ends.

2. Cut enough 2¼" (5.5 cm) × WOF (width-of fabric) strips to match that measurement.

3. Before you join the strips into one continuous strip, trim the ends with a 45-degree angle to miter the seams. Press the seams open.

4. Press the binding in half lengthwise with the wrong sides together.

5. Square up and trim the edges around the quilt before sewing the binding onto the quilt.

Sewing the Binding on the Quilt

NOTE: *Attach the binding to your quilt using the even-feed or walking foot on your sewing machine.*

6. Starting in the middle of one side, match the raw edges of the binding strips to the raw edges of the quilt top. Leave a 6" (15 cm) tail on the binding from where you start sewing. Starting with several backstitches, sew to the first corner and stop ¼" (6 mm) from the corner and backstitch.

7. Remove the quilt from the sewing machine, then fold the binding strips straight back from the corner and then at a 45-degree angle (FIGURE 1).

8. Holding the miter fold in place (and out of the way), align the binding strip with the next quilt edge. Continue sewing on the next edge (FIGURE 2).

9. Stitch around the quilt, finishing all the corners in the same manner. Stop about 4" (10 cm) from the starting point; remember to backstitch.

Joining the Binding Edges

10. Trim the tail, leaving it long enough to overlap the first unsewn tail by about 4–6" (10–15 cm). (FIGURE 3)

11. Unfold the binding of the extra length and cut, leaving a seam allowance at a 45-degree angle at the end of the first tail.

12. Lay the unfolded end of the tail under the angled tail. Draw a line on the unfolded tail alongside the cut edge.

13. Add a ½" (1.3 cm) seam allowance from the drawn line and trim (FIGURE 4).

14. Pin the angled tails right sides together and sew the binding ends together with a ¼" (6 mm) seam allowance (FIGURE 5). Press the seams open.

15. Refold the binding and continue sewing it on to the quilt's edge.

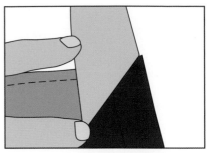

FIGURE 1

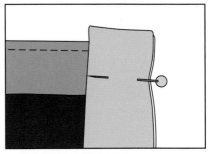

FIGURE 2

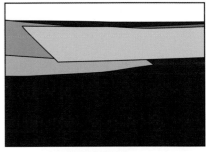

FIGURE 3

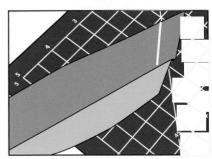

FIGURE 4

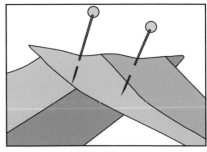

FIGURE 5

Finishing

16. Bring the folded edge of the binding to the back side of the quilt so that it covers the machine stitching.

17. Fold the unstitched binding at each corner to form a 45-degree mitered corner. Stitch from corner to corner of the binding.

NOTE: *The miter corner fold on the back and front should face the opposite directions from each other.*

18. Blind stitch the folded edge to the quilt back.

Labeling Your Quilt

Every quilt has a story and adding a label as the last step of the quilt-making process will help preserve the history of your quilt for future generations. The stories of many quilts have been lost because the maker did not take this important finishing step. Have fun and express your creativity with the label. Here are some tips on what to include on your label:

- Name of the quiltmaker
- Name of the quilt or quilt pattern
- Date the quilt was completed
- Place it was completed
- If the quilt is a gift, the recipient's name and the occasion
- Care instructions

CHAPTER 2

THE **BLOCKS**

Quilt blocks are the starting point for each of the projects in this book. The designs presented here are inspired by the red and white quilts in the International Quilt Study Center & Museum (IQSCM) collection. Each project is designed to be flexible, so blocks of the same size are interchangeable.

Block designs vary from very simple (Hourglass or Courthouse Steps, for example) to more complex (Touching Star). The blocks in this chapter are organized by size and technique and primarily shown with red designs on white background squares. Reversing the colors, so you have white designs on red squares, is easy and allows for even more variations on the projects shown in Chapter 3.

EACH PROJECT IS DESIGNED TO BE FLEXIBLE.

For this book, blocks were appliquéd with a popcorn/star stitch or a blanket stitch. See the stitch library available on your sewing machine and pick a design that reflects your style to vary the blocks even more.

Lobster

TECHNIQUE: Appliqué   FINISHED SIZE: 12" (30.5 cm) square

A unique name for an unusual appliqué design. This block was inspired by a quilt originating from the East Coast of the United States in the 1890s.

MATERIALS

☐ White fabric, 13" (33 cm) square

☐ Red fabric, 1 fat eighth (9" × 21" [23 cm × 53.5 cm])

☐ Paper-backed fusible webbing, ¼ yard (0.2 m)

☐ Red thread

☐ Lobster templates (on CD)

CUTTING INSTRUCTIONS

Follow manufacturer's instructions for fusing the paper-backed fusible web to the red fabric before cutting fabric.

From "pre-fused" red fabric, cut:

▸ 1 part A

▸ 4 part B

▸ 4 part C

BLOCK ASSEMBLY

Refer to FIGURE 1 throughout assembly.

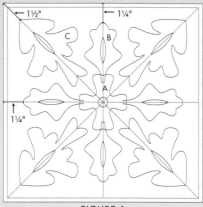

FIGURE 1

1. Locate the center of the white square by folding the fabric horizontally, vertically, and diagonally in both directions and creasing lightly (see Finding the Center of a Block in chapter 1).

2. Press 1 part B on each 90- and 180-degree fold line 1¼" (3.2 cm) from the edge.

3. Press part A in the center of the block overlapping the stem of each part B.

4. Press each part C on a diagonal line 1½" (3.8 cm) from corner.

5. Appliqué the shapes with your favorite stitch using red thread.

6. Using a rotary cutter and 12½" (31.5 cm) square ruler, trim the block to 12½" (31.5 cm) square. Once sewn in a quilt, the finished size is 12" (30.5 cm) square.

BLOCK ASSEMBLY

Refer to FIGURE 1 throughout assembly.

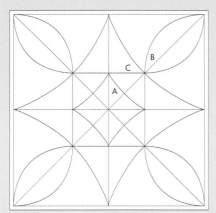

FIGURE 1

1. Locate the center of the white square by folding the fabric horizontally, vertically, and diagonally in both directions and creasing lightly (see Finding the Center of a Block in chapter 1).

2. Finger press part A in half vertically and horizontally to find the center. Press it in the middle of the white square.

3. Press each part C around part A, lining up the long edge as shown.

4. Press each part B on a vertical line ¼" (6 mm) from the corner.

5. Appliqué the shapes with your favorite stitch using red thread.

6. Using a rotary cutter and 12½" (31.5 cm) square ruler, trim the block to 12½" (31.5 cm) square. Once sewn in a quilt, the finished size is 12" (30.5 cm) square.

Cactus Flower

TECHNIQUE: Appliqué   FINISHED SIZE: 12" (30.5 cm) square

Cactus flowers offer a beautiful contrast to a very prickly plant. This appliqué block is interesting as a single block or when placed side by side without any setting strips to form a secondary pattern.

MATERIALS

☐ White fabric, (1) 13" (33 cm) square

☐ Red fabric, 1 fat eighth (9" × 21" [23 cm × 53.5 cm])

☐ Paper-backed fusible webbing, ¼ yard (0.2 m)

☐ Red thread

☐ Cactus flower templates (on CD)

CUTTING INSTRUCTIONS

Follow manufacturer's instructions for fusing the paper-backed fusible web to the red fabric before cutting fabric.

From "pre-fused" red fabric, cut:

▸ 1 part A

▸ 4 part B

▸ 4 part C

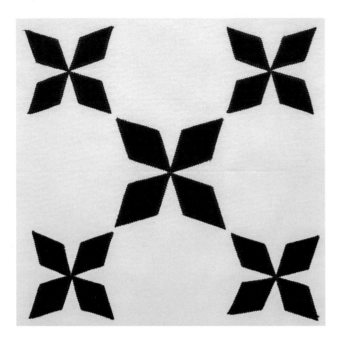

Diamonds

TECHNIQUE: Appliqué   FINISHED SIZE: 12" (30.5 cm) square

Diamonds are a popular shape for many pieced blocks. Here, they are featured as the main character in an appliqué motif. Although this block is very simple, it twinkles when used as part of a quilt design.

MATERIALS

- ☐ White fabric, 13" (33 cm) square
- ☐ Red fabric, 1 fat eighth (9" × 21" [23 cm × 53.5 cm])
- ☐ Paper-backed fusible webbing, ¼ yard (0.2 m)
- ☐ Red thread
- ☐ Diamond templates (on CD)

CUTTING INSTRUCTIONS

Follow manufacturer's instructions for fusing the paper-backed fusible web to the red fabric before cutting fabric.

From "pre-fused" red fabric, cut:

- ▸ 4 part A
- ▸ 16 part B

BLOCK ASSEMBLY

Refer to FIGURE 1 throughout assembly.

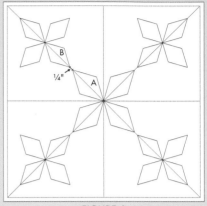

FIGURE 1

1. Locate the center of the white square by folding the fabric horizontally, vertically, and diagonally in both directions and creasing lightly (see Finding the Center of a Block in chapter 1).

2. Press each part A in the middle of the white square with the points centered on the diagonal lines.

3. Press 1 part B on each diagonal line ¼" (6 mm) from the tip of part A. Add the remaining diamonds in each grouping as shown with the points touching.

4. Appliqué the shapes with your favorite stitch using red thread.

5. Using a rotary cutter and 12½" (31.5 cm) square ruler, trim the block to 12½" (31.5 cm) square. Once sewn in a quilt, the finished size is 12" (30.5 cm) square.

BLOCK ASSEMBLY

Refer to FIGURE 1 throughout assembly.

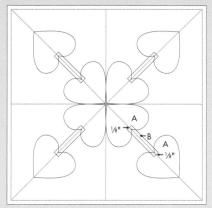

FIGURE 1

1. Locate the center of the white square by folding the fabric horizontally, vertically, and diagonally in both directions and creasing lightly (see Finding the Center of a Block in chapter 1).

2. Arrange 4 part A shapes along the diagonal lines in the center of the block.

3. Place the 4 part B or (4) ³⁄₈" × 2³⁄₈" (1 cm × 6 cm) rectangles ⅛" (3 mm) under the hearts on the diagonal lines. Press shapes in place.

4. Press the remaining part A shapes on the diagonal lines, overlapping the stems by ⅛" (3 mm).

5. Appliqué the shapes with your favorite stitch using red thread.

6. Using a rotary cutter and 12½" (31.5 cm) square ruler, trim the block to 12½" (31.5 cm) square. Once sewn in a quilt, the finished size is 12" (30.5 cm) square.

TIME-SAVER TIP

The following fabric cutting die can make the cutting process faster and more accurate:

- For Hearts, use GO! Heart 2", 3", 4" #55029

Eight of Hearts

TECHNIQUE: Appliqué   FINISHED SIZE: 12" (30.5 cm) square

With one of the meanings of the color red being love, it seems fitting that a design featuring hearts is presented for your enjoyment. The block design Eight of Hearts is also known as Sweethearts and Hearts and Darts.

MATERIALS

- ☐ White fabric, (1) 13" (33 cm) square
- ☐ Red fabric, 1 fat eighth (9" × 21" [23 cm × 53.5 cm])
- ☐ Paper-backed fusible webbing, ¼ yard (0.2 m)
- ☐ Red thread
- ☐ Eight of Hearts templates (on CD)

CUTTING INSTRUCTIONS

Follow manufacturer's instructions for fusing the paper-backed fusible web to the red fabric before cutting fabric.

From "pre-fused" red fabric, cut:

- ▸ 8 part A
- ▸ 4 part B or (4) ³⁄₈" × 2³⁄₈" (1 cm × 6 cm) rectangles

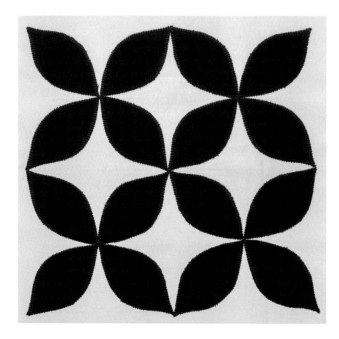

Four-Leaf Clover

TECHNIQUE: Appliqué   FINISHED SIZE: 12" (30.5 cm) square

Four-leaf clovers are considered good luck. Have you heard the myth that if you eat one a genie will appear? Although in this case, sewing one will reveal circles not genies.

MATERIALS

☐ White fabric, 13" (33 cm) square
☐ Red fabric, 1 fat eighth
  (9" × 21" [23 cm × 53.5 cm])
☐ Paper-backed fusible
  webbing, ¼ yard (0.2 m)
☐ Red thread
☐ Four-Leaf Clover template (on CD)

CUTTING INSTRUCTIONS

Follow manufacturer's instructions for fusing the paper-backed fusible web to the red fabric before cutting fabric.

From "pre-fused" red fabric, cut:

▸ 16 part A

BLOCK ASSEMBLY

1. Locate the center of the white square by folding the fabric horizontally, vertically, and diagonally in both directions and creasing lightly (see Finding the Center of a Block in chapter 1).

2. Press 4 part A shapes on the diagonal lines in the center of the white square with the ends touching (FIGURE 1).

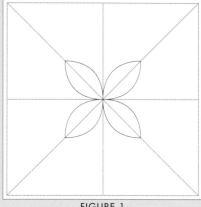

FIGURE 1

3. Using the center layout for placement, arrange the remaining part A shapes as shown (FIGURE 2). Press in place.

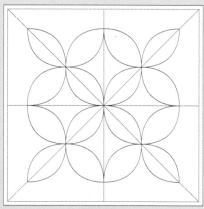

FIGURE 2

4. Appliqué the shapes with your favorite stitch using red thread.

5. Using a rotary cutter and 12½" (31.5 cm) square ruler, trim the block to 12½" (31.5 cm). Once sewn in a quilt, the finished size is 12" (30.5 cm) square.

Album
1850–1851
Maker Unknown
83" × 93" (211 cm × 236 cm)

Garden Maze

TECHNIQUE: Appliqué   FINISHED SIZE: 12" (30.5 cm) square

Also known as Tangled Garter and Sun Dial, this design is used in quilts both as a block and as a border treatment. The Garden Maze block is featured in a quilt from the 1890s that is in the International Quilt Study Center & Museum collection.

MATERIALS

- ☐ White fabric, (1) 13" (33 cm) square
- ☐ Red fabric, 1 fat eighth (9" × 21" [23 cm × 53.5 cm])
- ☐ Paper-backed fusible webbing, ¼ yard (0.2 m)
- ☐ Red thread
- ☐ Garden Maze templates (on CD)

CUTTING INSTRUCTIONS

Follow manufacturer's instructions for fusing the paper-backed fusible web to the red fabric before cutting fabric.

From "pre-fused" red fabric, cut:

- ▶ (3) ¾" × 21" (2 cm × 53.5 cm) strips; subcut (4) part A, (4) part B, and (4) part C
- ▶ (4) 1¼" × 21" (3.2 cm × 53.5 cm) strips; subcut (4) part D

BLOCK ASSEMBLY

1. Locate the center of the white square by folding the fabric horizontally, vertically, and diagonally in both directions and creasing lightly (see Finding the Center of a Block in chapter 1).

2. Press 4 part A shapes, forming a square in the center of the block (FIGURE 1).

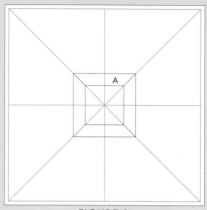

FIGURE 1

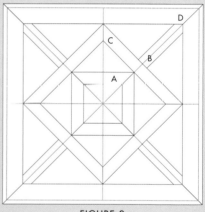

FIGURE 2

TIME-SAVER TIP

The following fabric cutting die can make the cutting process faster and more accurate:

- ■ For 1¼" (3.2 cm) strips, use GO! Strip Cutter #55109 1¼" (3.2 cm) [Finished ¾" (2 cm)]

3. Referring to FIGURE 2, position 4 part C shapes in a square as shown, then position the part B shapes on the diagonal lines. Press the shapes in place. Press the part D shapes along the edge of the square as shown.

NOTE: *Shapes will be ¼" (6 mm) from edge before trimming block.*

4. Appliqué the shapes with your favorite stitch using thread.

5. Using a rotary cutter and 12½" (31.5 cm) square ruler, trim the block to 12½" (31.5 cm). Once sewn in a quilt, the finished size is 12" (30.5 cm).

Garden Maze
1880–1900
Maker Unknown
79" × 87"
(200.5 cm × 221 cm)

Mirror Image

TECHNIQUE: Appliqué   FINISHED SIZE: 12" (30.5 cm) square

Inspired by a design from the 1850s, the repeating motifs in this appliqué make for a playful block.

1. Locate the center of the white square by folding the fabric horizontally, vertically, and diagonally in both directions and creasing lightly (see Finding the Center of a Block in chapter 1).

2. Press part A on the center line with the point 3½" (9 cm) from the bottom of the square.

3. Press part B 5" (12.5 cm) above the bottom point of part A.

4. Center part C directly under the edge of part B and press in place.

5. Arrange part D and part D reversed ¼" (6 mm) below the point of part A, slightly overlapping the ends of the handle. Arrange part F below the point of the heart 1" (2.5 cm) up from the bottom of the white square as shown. Arrange part E and part E reversed as shown with the ends under part D, part D reversed, and part F. Press the shapes in place.

MATERIALS

- ☐ White fabric, (1) 13" (33 cm) square
- ☐ Red fabric, 1 fat eighth (9" × 21" [23 cm × 53.5 cm])
- ☐ Paper-backed fusible webbing, ¼ yard (0.2 m)
- ☐ Red thread
- ☐ Mirror Image templates (on CD)

CUTTING INSTRUCTIONS

Follow manufacturer's instructions for fusing the paper-backed fusible web to the red fabric before cutting fabric.

From "pre-fused" red fabric, cut:

- ▸ (1) ¼" × 22" (6 mm × 56 cm) strip, subcut into (4) ¼" × 4" (6 mm × 10 cm) stems
- ▸ 1 part A
- ▸ 1 part B
- ▸ 1 part C
- ▸ 1 part D
- ▸ 1 part D, reversed
- ▸ 1 part E
- ▸ 1 part E, reversed
- ▸ 1 part F
- ▸ 12 part G

6. Press the end of each stem on a diagonal line ¾" (2 cm) from the corner and ¾" (2 cm) from the side edges. Curve the stems slightly as shown.

7. Press 3 part G shapes on each stem as shown.

8. Appliqué the shapes with your favorite stitch using red thread.

9. Using a rotary cutter and 12½" (31.5 cm) square ruler, trim the block to 12½" (31.5 cm) square. Once sewn in a quilt, the finished size is 12" (30.5 cm) square.

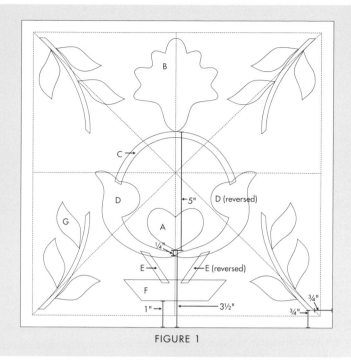

FIGURE 1

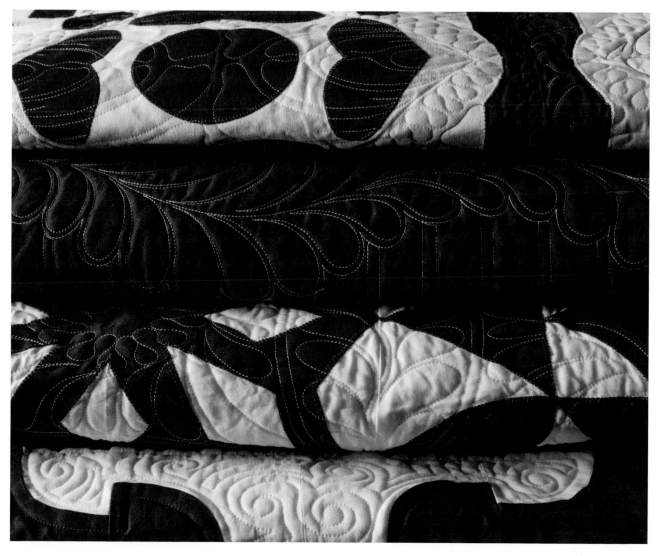

Oak Reel

TECHNIQUE: Appliqué   FINISHED SIZE: 12" (30.5 cm) square

Also known as Lovenulls Knot or Lovers Knot, this design has several variations. A Lovers Knot is a symbol of true love that cannot be separated and can be found in ancient Greece. It is thought that the expression "to tie the knot" when getting married is based on this symbol.

MATERIALS

☐ White fabric, 13" (33 cm) square
☐ Red fabric, 1 fat eighth
   (9" × 21" [23 cm × 53.5 cm])
☐ Paper-backed fusible
   webbing, ¼ yard (0.2 m)
☐ Red thread
☐ Oak Reel templates (on CD)

CUTTING INSTRUCTIONS

Follow manufacturer's instructions for fusing the paper-backed fusible web to the red fabric before cutting fabric.

From "pre-fused" red fabric, cut:

▸ 4 part A
▸ 4 part B
▸ 1 part C

BLOCK ASSEMBLY

Refer to FIGURE 1 throughout assembly.

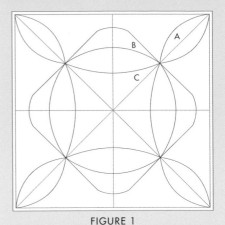

FIGURE 1

1. Locate the center of the white square by folding the fabric horizontally, vertically, and diagonally in both directions and creasing lightly (see Finding the Center of a Block in chapter 1).

2. Fold part C in half lengthwise and horizontally to find the center. Press it in the center of the white square.

3. Press the part B shapes in place as shown.

4. Fold the part A shapes in half lengthwise. Place them on the diagonals so they touch the corners of part C.

5. Appliqué the shapes with your favorite stitch using red thread.

6. Using a rotary cutter and 12½" (31.5 cm) square ruler, trim the block to 12½" (30.5 cm) square. Once sewn in a quilt, the finished size is 12" (30.5 cm) square.

BLOCK ASSEMBLY

Refer to FIGURE 1 throughout assembly.

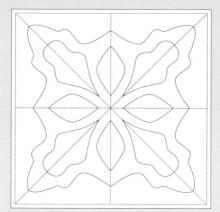

FIGURE 1

1. Locate the center of the white square by folding the fabric horizontally, vertically, and diagonally in both directions and creasing lightly (see Finding the Center of a Block in chapter 1).

2. Center part A in the middle of the white square and press in place.

3. Appliqué the shape with your favorite stitch using red thread.

4. Using a rotary cutter and 12½" (31.5 cm) square ruler, trim the block to 12½" (31.5 cm) square. Once sewn in a quilt, the finished size is 12" (30.5 cm) square.

Paper Cut

TECHNIQUE: Appliqué   FINISHED SIZE: 12" (30.5 cm) square

The art of paper cutting dates back to the sixth century. By the mid-1800s the look of this intricate art form had become popular in quilting. This block is inspired by the Album quilt in the International Quilt Study Center & Museum collection, which was made in Boston, Massachusetts, between 1850 and 1851.

MATERIALS

☐ White fabric, (1) 13" (33 cm) square

☐ Red fabric, 1 fat quarter (18" × 21" [23 cm × 53.5 cm])

☐ Paper-backed fusible webbing, ¼ yard (0.2 m)

☐ Red thread

☐ Paper Cut templates (on CD)

CUTTING INSTRUCTIONS

Follow manufacturer's instructions for fusing the paper-backed fusible web to the red fabric before cutting fabric.

From "pre-fused" red fabric, cut:

▸ 1 template A

Snowflake

TECHNIQUE: Appliqué FINISHED SIZE: 12" (30.5 cm) square

The symmetrical design of this block reminds me of the German paper art known as *scherenschnitte,* which translates to "scissor cut." Traditionally, the designs depicted people and animals or told a story. In this application, the shape makes me think of a cold wintery day and the beauty that is seen in a single snowflake.

MATERIALS

- ☐ White fabric, 13" (33 cm) square
- ☐ Red fabric, 1 fat eighth (9" x 21" [23 cm x 53.5 cm])
- ☐ Paper-backed fusible webbing, ¼ yard (0.2 m)
- ☐ Red thread
- ☐ Snowflake template (on CD)

CUTTING INSTRUCTIONS

Follow manufacturer's instructions for fusing the paper-backed fusible web to the red fabric before cutting fabric.

From "pre-fused" red fabric, cut:

▸ 1 part A

BLOCK ASSEMBLY

Refer to FIGURE 1 throughout assembly.

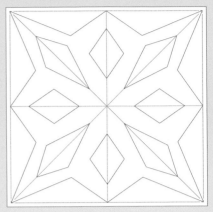

FIGURE 1

1. Locate the center of the white square by folding the fabric horizontally, vertically, and diagonally in both directions, creasing lightly (see Finding the Center of a Block in chapter 1). Using a fabric pencil, lightly draw a line ⅜" (1 cm) diagonally from each corner. These are the guidelines for the points of the snowflake.

2. Press 1 snowflake in the center of the white square using the pencil guidelines.

3. Appliqué the shapes with your favorite stitch using matching thread.

4. Using a rotary cutter and 12½" (31.5 cm) square ruler, trim the block to 12½" (31.5 cm) square. Once sewn in a quilt, the finished size is 12" (30.5 cm) square.

BLOCK ASSEMBLY

Refer to FIGURE 1 throughout assembly.

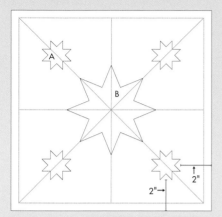

FIGURE 1

1. Locate the center of the white square by folding the fabric horizontally, vertically, and diagonally in both directions and creasing lightly (see Finding the Center of a Block in chapter 1).

2. Finger press part B in half lengthwise and horizontally to find the center. Press part B in the center of the block.

3. Press each part A on a diagonal line 1¾" (4.5 cm) from the sides as shown.

4. Appliqué the shapes with your favorite stitch using matching thread.

5. Using a rotary cutter and 12½" (31.5 cm) square ruler, trim the block to 12½" (31.5 cm) square. Once sewn in a quilt, the finished size is 12" (30.5 cm) square.

Stars

TECHNIQUE: Appliqué   FINISHED SIZE: 12" (30.5 cm) square

Stars, both appliquéd and pieced, are some of the most popular motifs in quilting. This simple design lets them shine!

MATERIALS

☐ White fabric, (1) 13" (33 cm) square
☐ Red fabric, 1 fat eighth (9" × 21" [23 cm × 53.5 cm])
☐ Paper-backed fusible webbing, ¼ yard (0.2 m)
☐ Red thread
☐ Star templates (on CD)

CUTTING INSTRUCTIONS

Follow manufacturer's instructions for fusing the paper-backed fusible web to the red fabric before cutting fabric.

From "pre-fused" red fabric, cut:

▸ 4 part A
▸ 1 part B

Sunburst

TECHNIQUE: Appliqué   FINISHED SIZE: 12" (30.5 cm) square

Originally, the Sunburst block was pieced and limited to experienced quilters because of its complexity. Created here using appliqué, it is much easier to execute and just as striking, making it a great block for quilters of all skill levels.

MATERIALS

☐ White fabric, 13" (33 cm) square
☐ Red fabric, 1 fat eighth
   (9" × 21" [23 cm × 53.5 cm])
☐ Paper-backed fusible
   webbing, ¼ yard (0.2 m)
☐ Red thread
☐ Sunburst templates (on CD)

CUTTING INSTRUCTIONS

Follow manufacturer's instructions for fusing the paper-backed fusible web to the red fabric before cutting fabric.

From "pre-fused" red fabric, cut:

▸ 12 part A
▸ 1 part B

BLOCK ASSEMBLY

1. Locate the center of the block by folding the fabric square in half twice. From the center, use the 30 degree lines on your quilting ruler to mark the block as shown (FIGURE 1).

2. Referring to FIGURE 2, press part B in the center of the block as shown.

3. Press each part A on the diamond placement lines with the tips touching the outside of the circle.

4. Appliqué the shapes with your favorite stitch using red thread.

5. Using a rotary cutter and 12½" (31.5 cm) square ruler, trim the block to 12½" (31.5 cm) square. Once sewn in a quilt, the finished size is 12" (30.5 cm) square.

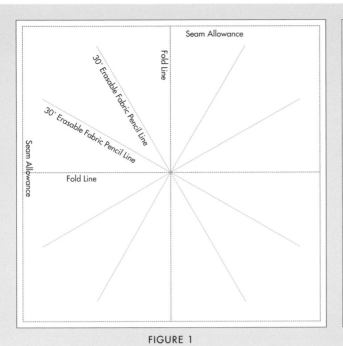

FIGURE 1

FIGURE 2

- (1) 6¼" × 12½" (16 cm × 31.5 cm) rectangle for handle background
- (1) 2" × 12½" (5 cm × 31.5 cm) rectangle for bottom background strip
- (2) 1½" × 4¾" (3.8 cm × 12 cm) rectangles for base background strip
- (2) 1½" × 4¼" (3.8 cm × 11 cm) rectangles for side background strips
- (1) 4⅝" (11.5 cm) square; subcut in half diagonally to make (2) half-square triangles for basket background triangles
- (1) 2⅝" × 21" (6.5 cm × 53.5 cm) strip; subcut (3) 2⅝" (6.5 cm) squares; cut squares in half diagonally to make (6) half-square triangles for basket
- (1) 1⅞" (5 cm) square; subcut in half diagonally to make (2) half-square triangles for basket-base background triangles

From red fabric, cut:

- (1) 2⅝" × 21" (6.5 cm × 53.5 cm) strip; subcut (5) 2⅝" (6.5 cm) squares; cut squares in half diagonally to make (10) half-square triangles for basket
- (1) 1⅞" (4.5 cm) square; cut in half diagonally to make (2) half-square triangles for basket base
- (1) 1½" × 3" (3.8 cm × 7.5 cm) rectangle for basket base

From "pre-fused" red fabric, cut:

- 1 part A

Basket

TECHNIQUE: Appliqué and Piecing   FINISHED SIZE: 12" (30.5 cm) square

Baskets of all shapes and sizes have been loved for generations. Baskets are useful as well as decorative, so it is not surprising that they have become popular motifs on quilt blocks.

MATERIALS

- ☐ White fabric, 13" (33 cm) square
- ☐ Red fabric, 1 fat eighth (9" × 21" [23 cm × 53.5 cm])
- ☐ Paper-backed fusible webbing, ¼ yard (0.2 m)
- ☐ Red thread
- ☐ Basket template (on CD)

CUTTING INSTRUCTIONS

Follow manufacturer's instructions for fusing the paper-backed fusible web to the red fabric before cutting fabric.

From white fabric, cut:

- (1) 2⅝" × 21" (6.5 cm × 53.5 cm) strips; subcut (3) 2⅝" (6.5 cm) squares; cut squares in half diagonally to make (6) half-square triangles

BLOCK ASSEMBLY

1. Sew together 1 red and 1 white 2⅝" (6.5 cm) half-square triangle (FIGURE 1) to make a Half-Square Triangle unit. Trim dog-ears and press seams open. Make 5 units.

2. Sew together (1) 1⅞" (5 cm) red half-square triangle and (1) 1⅞" (5 cm) white half-square triangle. Trim dog-ears and press seams open. Make 2 Half-Square Triangle units for the basket base.

3. Referring to FIGURE 2, sew together 2 Half-Square Triangle units, then sew a red triangle to the top and a white triangle to the bottom. Sew together 2 Half-Square Triangle units, then sew a red triangle to the top. Sew a red triangle to the top of a Half-Square Triangle unit, then sew a red triangle to the white side. Finally, sew the diagonal rows together to make the Basket unit.

4. Referring to FIGURE 3, sew (1) 4⅝" (11.5 cm) white half-square triangle to each side of the Basket unit. Then sew (1) 1½" × 4¼" (3.8 cm × 11 cm) rectangle to the short sides of the Basket unit.

5. To make the Basket Base unit, sew (1) 1⅞" (5 cm) Half-Square Triangle unit to the short sides of the 1½" × 3" (3.8 cm × 7.5 cm) red rectangle. Add (1) 1½" × 4¾" (3.8 cm × 12 cm) white rectangle to each side of the row (FIGURE 4).

6. Referring to FIGURE 5, sew (1) 2" × 12½" (5 cm × 31.5 cm) white rectangle to the bottom of the basket row. Sew the Basket Base unit to the bottom of the Basket unit. Then sew the 6¼" × 12½" (16 cm × 31.5 cm) white rectangle to top of the Basket unit.

7. Fuse part A in place as shown (FIGURE 6). Appliqué the handle with your favorite stitch using red thread.

8. Using a rotary cutter and 12½" (31.5 cm) square ruler, trim the block to 12½" (31.5 cm) square. Once sewn in a quilt, the finished size is 12" (30.5 cm) square.

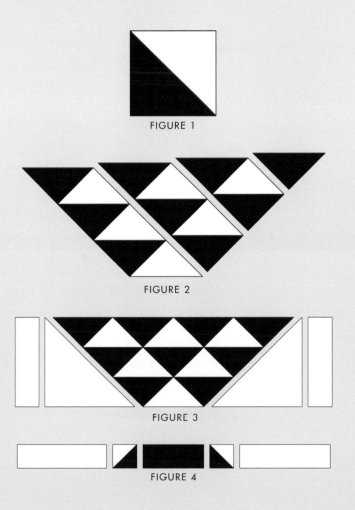

FIGURE 1

FIGURE 2

FIGURE 3

FIGURE 4

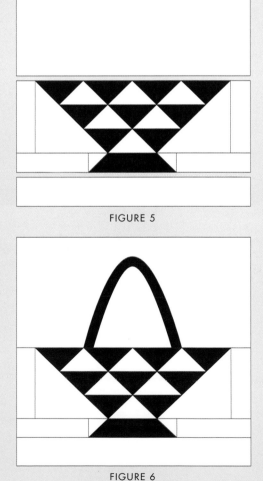

FIGURE 5

FIGURE 6

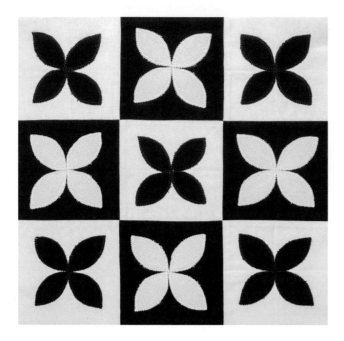

Nine Patch with Leaves

TECHNIQUES: Appliqué and Piecing FINISHED SIZE: 12" (30.5 cm) square

The Nine Patch block is one of the most popular blocks in quilt designs. Here, leaves are appliquéd on the blocks to add interest to a simple design.

BLOCK ASSEMBLY

1. Sew the 4½" (11.5 cm) red and white squares together as shown (FIGURE 1). Press the seams open.

2. Sew the rows together. Press the seams open.

3. Referring to FIGURE 2, center 4 same-color leaves on the opposite color square on a 45–degree angle. Press in place.

4. Appliqué the leaves to the square using your favorite stitch, matching the thread to the leaf color.

5. Using a rotary cutter and 12½" (31.5 cm) square ruler, trim the block to 12½" (31.5 cm) square. Once sewn in a quilt, the finished size is 12" (30.5 cm) square.

TIME-SAVER TIP

The following fabric cutting die can make the cutting process faster and more accurate:

- For 4½" (11.5 cm) squares, use GO! Value Die #55018

MATERIALS

- ☐ White fabric, 1 fat eighth (9" × 21" [23 cm × 53.5 cm])
- ☐ Red fabric, 1 fat eighth (9" × 21" [23 cm × 53.5 cm])
- ☐ Paper-backed fusible web, ⅛ yard (0.1 m)
- ☐ Red and white thread
- ☐ Nine Patch with Leaves templates (on CD)

CUTTING INSTRUCTIONS

Follow manufacturer's instructions for fusing the paper-backed fusible web to the red fabric before cutting fabric.

From white fabric, cut:

▸ (1) 4½" (11.4 cm) × WOF (width-of-fabric) strip; subcut into (5) 4½" (11.5 cm) squares

From "pre-fused" white fabric, cut:

▸ 16 part A

From red fabric, cut:

▸ (1) 4½" (11.5 cm) × WOF strip; subcut into (4) 4½" (11.5 cm) squares

From "pre-fused" red fabric, cut:

▸ 20 part A

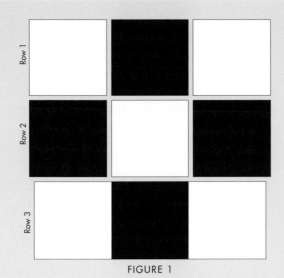

FIGURE 1

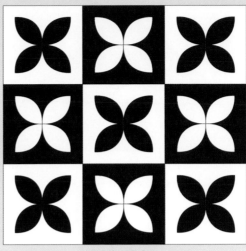

FIGURE 2

Nine Patch
Maker Unknown
1890–1910
35" × 58½"
(90 cm × 149 cm)

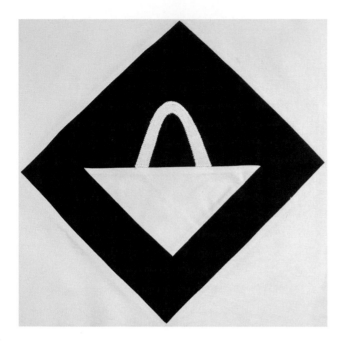

Small Basket

TECHNIQUES: Appliqué and Piecing   FINISHED SIZE: 12" (30.5 cm) square

Baskets come in all shapes and sizes and so do basket designs on quilt blocks. Made from a basic half-square triangle block, this basket is simple and adorable.

BLOCK ASSEMBLY

1. Sew together 1 red and 1 white 5½" (14 cm) half-square triangle. Trim dog-ears and press the seam open. The Half-Square Triangle unit should measure 5⅛" (13 cm) (FIGURE 1).

2. Referring to FIGURE 2, sew (1) 2½" × 5⅛" (6.5 cm × 13 cm) red rectangle to 2 opposite sides of the Half-Square Triangle unit. Press the seams open. Then sew (1) 2½" × 9" (6.5 cm × 23 cm) red rectangle to the remaining sides. Press the seams open.

3. Sew a 6⅞" (17.5 cm) white half-square triangle to each corner (FIGURE 3). Press seams open.

4. Press part A in place (FIGURE 4). Appliqué with your favorite stitch using white thread.

5. Using a rotary cutter and 12½" (31.5 cm) square ruler, trim the block to 12½" (31.5 cm) square. Once sewn in a quilt, the finished size is 12" (30.5 cm) square.

MATERIALS

- ☐ White fabric, 1 fat eighth (9" × 21" [23 cm × 53.5 cm])
- ☐ Red fabric, 1 fat eighth (9" × 21" [23 cm × 53.5 cm])
- ☐ Paper-backed fusible web, 4" (10 cm) square
- ☐ White thread
- ☐ Small Basket template (on CD)

CUTTING INSTRUCTIONS

Follow manufacturer's instructions for fusing the paper-backed fusible web to the "pre-fused" white fabric before cutting fabric.

From white fabric, cut:

- ▸ (1) 5½" (14 cm) square; subcut diagonally into 2 half-square triangles
- ▸ (2) 6⅞" (17.5 cm) squares; subcut each square diagonally into 2 half-square triangles

From "pre-fused" white fabric, cut:

- ▸ 1 part A

From red fabric, cut:

- ▸ (1) 4" (10 cm) square for the handle
- ▸ (1) 5½" (14 cm) square; subcut diagonally into 2 half-square triangles
- ▸ (2) 2½" (6.5 cm) × WOF (width-of-fabric) strips; subcut each into (1) 2½" × 5⅛ (6.5 cm × 13 cm) and (1) 2½" × 9" (6.5 cm × 23 cm) strips for the borders

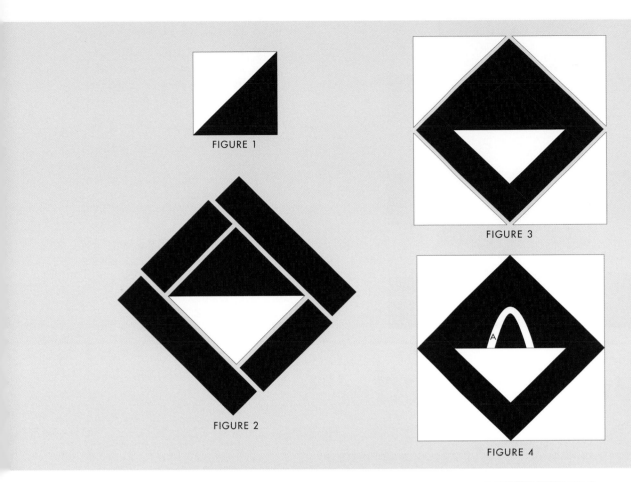

FIGURE 1

FIGURE 3

FIGURE 2

FIGURE 4

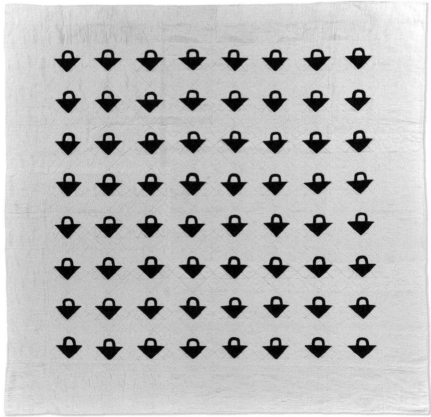

Basket
1900–1920
Maker Unknown
67" × 68"
(170 cm × 173 cm)

Checkerboard

TECHNIQUE: Piecing   FINISHED SIZE: 12" (30.5 cm) square

Using just solid colors, the Checkerboard block is easy to make yet striking and bold. The game of Checkers or Draughts, as it is called in England, dates back to ancient times.

MATERIALS

☐ White fabric, ¼ yard (0.2 m)
☐ Red fabric, ¼ yard (0.2 m)
☐ Red and white thread

CUTTING INSTRUCTIONS

From white fabric, cut:

▸ (3) 2½" (6.5 cm) × WOF (width-of-fabric) strips

From red fabric, cut:

▸ (3) 2½" (6.5 cm) × WOF strips

BLOCK ASSEMBLY

1. Sew red and white strips together along the long edges as shown (FIGURE 1). Press the seams open. Make 2 strip sets.

2. Cross cut the strip set into (6) 2½" (6.5 cm) wide segments (FIGURE 2).

3. Referring to FIGURE 3, arrange the rows as shown. Sew the rows together and press the seams open.

4. Square up the block to 12½" (31.5 cm) square. Once sewn in a quilt, the finished size is 12" (30.5 cm) square.

TIME-SAVER TIP

The following fabric cutting die can make the cutting process faster and more accurate:

■ For 2½" (6.5 cm) strips, use GO! Strip Cutter #55017 2½" (6.5 cm) [Finished 2" (5 cm)]

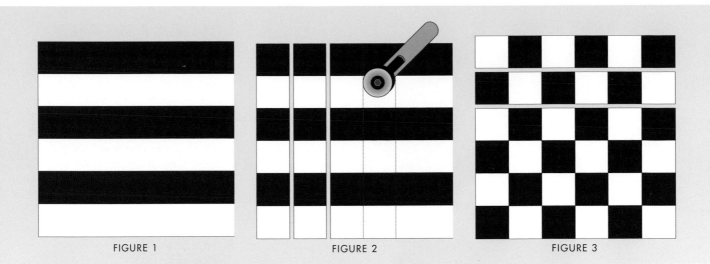

FIGURE 1   FIGURE 2   FIGURE 3

The Childhood Games Quilt features a playful mix of Checkerboard and Snowball blocks.

Chimney Sweep

TECHNIQUE: Piecing   FINISHED SIZE: 12" (30.5 cm) square

Also known as an Album block, the Chimney Sweep block was sometimes used when signatures were added to a quilt. These quilts were often given as gifts or used for fundraising. When used for fund-raising, a person would need to "purchase" the space in order to have their name on the quilt.

MATERIALS

☐ White fabric, 1 fat quarter
(18" × 21" [45.5 cm × 53.5 cm])

☐ Red fabric, 1 fat eighth
(9" × 21" [23 cm × 53.5 cm])

☐ Red and white thread

CUTTING INSTRUCTIONS

From white fabric, cut:

▸ (2) 2⅝" × 21" (6.5 cm × 53.5 cm) strips; subcut (2) 2⅝" (6.5 cm) squares and (1) 2⅝" × 7" (6.5 cm × 18 cm) rectangle

▸ (1) 4¼" (11 cm) × WOF (width-of-fabric) strip; subcut (3) 4¼" (11 cm) squares; cut each square in half diagonally twice to make 12 quarter-square triangles

▸ (2) 3" (7.5 cm) squares; subcut squares in half diagonally to make 4 half-square triangles

From red fabric, cut:

▸ (2) 2⅜" × 21" (6 cm × 53.5 cm) strips; subcut (8) 2⅝" (6.5 cm) squares and (4) 2⅝" × 7" (6.5 cm × 18 cm) rectangles

BLOCK ASSEMBLY

1. Sew (2) 3⅜" (8.5 cm) white quarter-square triangles to opposite sides of (1) 2⅝" (6.5 cm) red square. Sew (1) 3" (7.5 cm) white half-square triangle to one side to complete the Corner unit (FIGURE 1). Trim dog-ears and press seams open. Make 4 Corner units.

2. Sew (1) 3⅜" (8.5 cm) white quarter-square triangle to each short side of (1) 2⅝" × 7" (6.5 cm × 18 cm) red rectangle (FIGURE 2). Press seams open. Make 2 Row units.

3. Sew together 1 Corner unit and 1 Row unit (FIGURE 3). Trim dog-ears and press seams open. Make 2 large Corner units.

4. Referring to FIGURE 4, sew together (1) 2⅝" (6.5 cm) red square, (1) 2⅝" (6.5 cm) white square, and (1) 2⅝" (6.5 cm) red square. Make 2 rows. Sew 1 pieced row to each long side of the 2⅝" × 7" (6.5 cm × 18 cm) white rectangle. Sew (1) 2⅝" × 7" (6.5 cm × 18 cm) red rectangle to each side of the Center unit as shown. Press the seams opens.

5. Arrange the units as shown (FIGURE 5), then sew them together (FIGURE 6). Press the seams open.

6. Square up the block to 12½" (31.5 cm) square. Once sewn in a quilt, the finished size is 12" (30.5 cm) square.

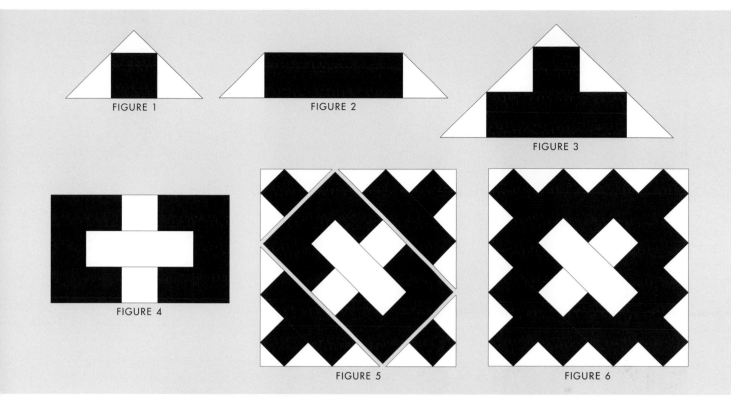

FIGURE 1

FIGURE 2

FIGURE 3

FIGURE 4

FIGURE 5

FIGURE 6

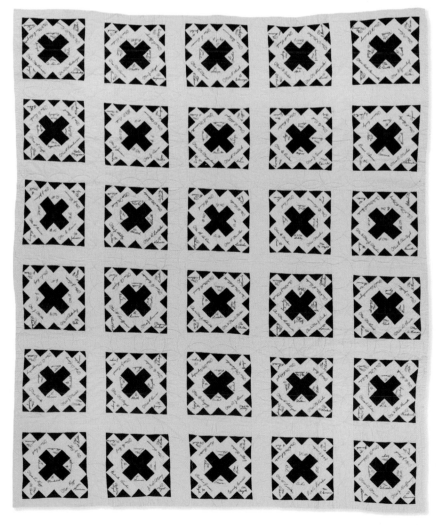

Friendship Chain
Circa 1898
Maker: Lydia Schuette
73¾" × 91¼"
(187 cm × 232 cm)

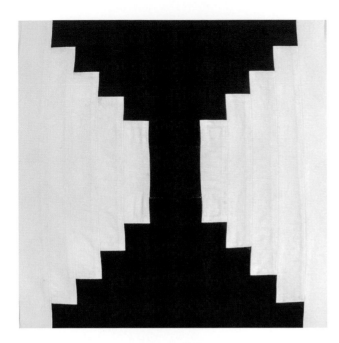

Courthouse Steps

TECHNIQUE: Piecing   FINISHED SIZE: 12" (30.5 cm) square

A variation of the beginner-friendly Log Cabin block, Courthouse Steps is very eye-catching, especially in this red-and-white color scheme.

MATERIALS

- ☐ White fabric, 1 fat quarter (18" × 21" [23 cm × 53.5 cm])
- ☐ Red fabric, 1 fat quarter (18" × 21" [23 cm × 53.5 cm])
- ☐ Red and white thread

CUTTING INSTRUCTIONS

From white fabric, cut:

- ▸ (4) 1½" × 21" (3.8 × 53.5 cm) strips, subcut into (2) 1½" × 4½" (3.8 cm × 11.5 cm), (2) 1½" × 6½" (3.8 cm × 16.5 cm), (2)1½" × 8½" (3.8 cm × 21.5 cm), (2) 1½" × 10½" (3.8 cm × 26.5 cm), and (2) 1½" × 12½" (3.8 cm × 31.5 cm) rectangles

From red fabric, cut:

- ▸ (1) 2½" (6.5 cm) square for piece 1

- ▸ (5) 1½" × 21" (3.8 cm × 53.5 cm) strips; subcut into (2) 1½" × 2½" (3.8 cm × 6.5 cm), (2) 1½" × 4½" (3.8 cm × 11.5 cm), (2) 1½" × 6½" (3.8 cm × 16.5 cm), (2) 1½" × 8½" (3.8 cm × 21.5 cm), and (2) 1½" × 10½" (3.8 cm × 26.5 cm) rectangles

BLOCK ASSEMBLY

Press seams open as you sew.

1. Lay out the strips as shown (FIGURE 1).

2. Referring to FIGURE 2, sew (1) 1½" × 2½" (3.8 cm × 6.5 cm) red log to opposite sides of the 2½" (6.5 cm) red square. Sew (1) 1½" × 4½" (3.8 cm × 11.5 cm) white log to opposite sides of the Center unit.

3. Sew (1) 1½" × 4½" (3.8 cm × 11.5 cm) red log to the top and bottom of the Center unit (FIGURE 3). Continue joining the logs as shown, working your way around the block sewing white logs to white logs and red logs to red logs (FIGURE 4).

4. Square up the block to 12½" (31.5 cm) square. Once sewn in a quilt, the finished size is 12" (30.5 cm) square.

TIME-SAVER TIP

The following fabric cutting dies can make the cutting process faster and more accurate:

- ■ For 1½" (3.8 cm) for logs, use GO! Strip Cutter #55024 1½" (3.8 cm) [Finished 1" (2.5 cm)]
- ■ For 2½" (6.5 cm) squares, use GO! Square #55059 2½" (6.5 cm) Multiples [Finished 2" (5 cm)]

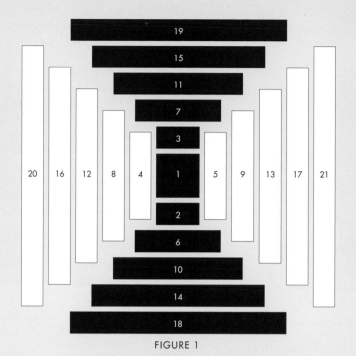

FIGURE 1

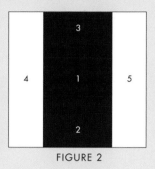

FIGURE 2

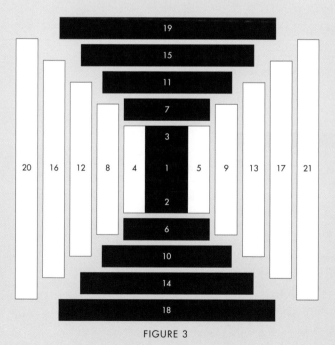

FIGURE 3

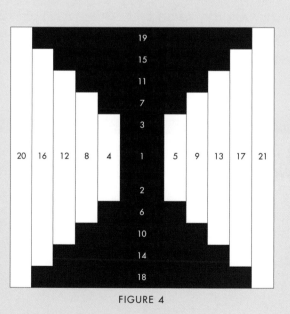

FIGURE 4

Crossroads

TECHNIQUE: Piecing   FINISHED SIZE: 12" (30.5 cm) square

It is easy to understand how this block got its name. However, the name could have multiple meanings: A community of people smaller than a village, a crisis, or a point where a decision needs to be made. Hopefully, the decision you make is to use this block in your next project.

MATERIALS

☐ White fabric, 1 fat quarter (18" × 21" [23 cm × 53.5 cm])

☐ Red fabric, 1 fat eighth (9" × 21" [23 cm × 53.5 cm])

☐ Red and white thread

CUTTING INSTRUCTIONS

From white fabric, cut:

▸ (2) 2⅜" (6 cm) squares; subcut in half diagonally to make 4 half-square triangles

▸ (1) 2½" (6.5 cm) square

▸ (1) 10½" (26.5 cm) square; subcut in half diagonally twice to make 4 quarter-square triangles

From red fabric, cut:

▸ (2) 2½" × 21" (6.5 cm × 53.5 cm) strips; subcut into (4) 2½" × 7" (6.5 cm × 18 cm) rectangles

BLOCK ASSEMBLY

Refer to Figure 1 throughout assembly. Press seams open as you sew.

1. Sew (1) 10½" (26.5 cm) white quarter-square triangle to each long side of (1) 2½" × 7" (6.5 cm × 18 cm) red rectangle. Make 2 units.

2. Sew 1 small white half-square triangle to the bottom of each unit.

3. To make the center row, sew (1) 2½" × 7" (6.5 cm × 18 cm) red rectangle to opposite sides of the 2½" (6.5 cm) white square. On each end, sew 1 small white half-square triangle.

4. Sew the rows together to complete the block (FIGURE 2).

5. Square up the block to 12½" (31.5 cm) square. Once sewn in a quilt, the finished size is 12" (30.5 cm) square.

TIME-SAVER TIP

The following fabric cutting dies can make the cutting process faster and more accurate:

■ For 2½" (6.5 cm) strips, use GO! Strip Cutter #55017 2½" (6.5 cm) [Finished 2" (5 cm)]

■ For 2½" (6.5 cm) squares, use GO! Square #55059 2½" (6.5 cm) Multiples [Finished 2" (5 cm)]

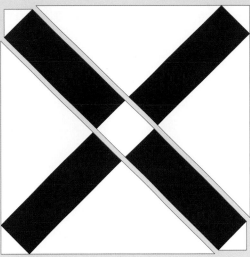

FIGURE 1

FIGURE 2

Red squares add a dramatic contrast to
the Crossroads and Wild Goose Chase
blocks in the X Marks the Spot Quilt.

Hourglass

TECHNIQUE: Piecing   FINISHED SIZE: 12" (30.5 cm) square

This shape is often used as a unit within a block to create a more complicated design, but it can also be used on its own to add a graphic element to any quilt.

MATERIALS

☐ White fabric, 1 fat quarter (18" × 21" [23 cm × 53.5 cm])

☐ Red fabric, 1 fat quarter (18" × 21" [23 cm × 53.5 cm])

☐ Red and white thread

CUTTING INSTRUCTIONS

From white fabric, cut:

▸ (1) 13¼" (33.5 cm) square; sub-cut diagonally twice to create 4 quarter-square triangles

From red fabric, cut:

▸ (1) 13¼" (33.5 cm) square; sub-cut diagonally twice to create 4 quarter-square triangles

BLOCK ASSEMBLY

Refer to FIGURE 1 throughout assembly.

FIGURE 1

1. Sew together 1 white quarter-square triangle and 1 red quarter-square triangle to form half of the Quarter-Square unit. Make 2 units. Press the seams open.

2. Sew the 2 halves together to complete the block, alternating the positions of the red and white triangles. Trim dog-ears and press seams open.

3. Square up the block to 12½" (31.5 cm) square. Once sewn in a quilt, the finished size is 12" (30.5 cm) square.

Hour Glass
1890–1990
Maker Unknown
15" × 17½"
(38 cm x 44.5 cm)

Five Quarter-Squares

TECHNIQUE: Piecing   FINISHED SIZE: 12" (30.5 cm) square

The quarter-square is a basic building block in quiltmaking. Here, the shape is used five times to create a bold and sharp design.

TIME-SAVER TIP

The following fabric cutting dies can make the cutting process faster and more accurate:

- For 3½" × 6½" (9 cm × 16.5 cm) rectangles, Use GO! Rectangle #55002 3½" × 6½" (9 cm × 16.5 cm) [Finished 3" × 6" (7.5 cm × 15 cm)]

- For 6½" (16.5 cm) quarter-squares triangles, use GO! Quarter Square Triangle #55002 [6" (15 cm) Finished Square]

- For 3½" (6.5 cm) quarter-squares triangles, use GO! Quarter Square Triangle #55396 [3" (7.5 cm) Finished Square]

MATERIALS

- ☐ White fabric, 1 fat quarter (18" × 21" [45.5 cm × 53.5 cm])
- ☐ Red fabric, 1 fat quarter (18" × 21" [45.5 cm × 53.5 cm])
- ☐ Red and white thread

CUTTING INSTRUCTIONS

From white fabric, cut:

- ▸ (1) 7¼" (18.5 cm) square; sub-cut diagonally twice to make 4 quarter-square triangles

- ▸ (1) 4¼" × 21" (11 cm × 53.5 cm) strip; subcut (2) 4¼" (11 cm) squares, then cut squares diagonally twice to make 8 quarter-square triangles

- ▸ (1) 3½" × 21" (9 cm × 53.5 cm) strip; subcut (2) 3½" × 6½" (9 cm × 16.5 cm) rectangles

From red fabric, cut:

- ▸ (1) 7¼" (18.5 cm) square; sub-cut diagonally twice to create 4 quarter-square triangles

- ▸ (1) 4¼" × 21" (11 cm × 53.5 cm) strip; subcut (2) 4¼" (11 cm) squares, then cut squares diagonally twice to make 8 quarter-square triangles

- ▸ (1) 3½" × 21" (9 cm × 53.5 cm) strip; subcut (2) 3½" × 6½" (9 cm × 16.5 cm) rectangles

BLOCK ASSEMBLY

1. Referring to FIGURE 1, sew together (1) 7¼" (18.5 cm) white quarter-square triangle and (1) 7¼" (18.5 cm) red quarter-square triangle to form half of the large Quarter-Square unit. Trim dog-ears and press seams open. Make 2 units, alternating the positions of the red and white triangles.

2. Sew the large Quarter-Square units together to form the Center unit. Press the seams open. The large Quarter-Square unit should measure 6½" (16.5 cm) square (FIGURE 2).

3. Sew together (1) 4¼" (11 cm) white quarter-square triangle and (1) 4¼" (11 cm) red quarter-square triangle to form half of the small Quarter-Square unit. Press the seam open. Make 8 units.

4. Sew 2 small Quarter-Square units together. Trim dog ears and press the seams open. The small Quarter-Square units should measure 3½" (9 cm). Make 4 small corner Quarter-Square units, alternating the positions of the red and white triangles. Press seams open.

NOTE: Refer to FIGURE 3 for steps 5–7.

5. Sew (1) 3½" × 6½" (9 cm × 16.5 cm) white rectangle to each of the red sides of the large Quarter-Square unit. Press seams open.

6. Sew 1 small Quarter-Square unit to each end of a 3½" × 6½" (9 cm × 16.5 cm) red rectangle, matching the white sides to the small end of the red rectangle. Make 2 rows. Press seams open.

7. Arrange the rows of the block as shown. Sew the rows together (FIGURE 3) and press the seams open.

8. Square up the block to 12½" (31.5 cm) square. Once sewn in a quilt, the finished size is 12" (30.5 cm) square.

FIGURE 1

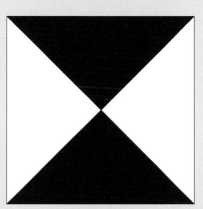

FIGURE 2

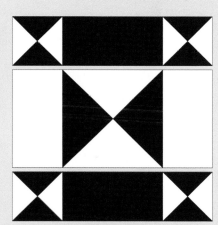

FIGURE 3

Ohio Star

TECHNIQUE: Piecing   FINISHED SIZE: 12" (30.5 cm) square

Dating back to the 1800s, the Ohio Star block has been a favorite for generations. Based on a Nine Patch block setting with quarter-squares, it is simple, graphic, and appealing.

TIME-SAVER TIP

The following fabric cutting dies can make the cutting process faster and more accurate:

- For 4½" (11.5 cm) squares, use GO! Value Die #55018
- For 4½" (11.5 cm) Half-Square Triangles, use GO! Half Square Triangle #55031 [4" (10 cm) Finished Square]

MATERIALS

- ☐ White fabric, 1 fat quarter (18" × 21" [23 cm × 53.5 cm])
- ☐ Red fabric, 1 fat quarter (18" × 21" [23 cm × 53.5 cm])
- ☐ Red and white thread

CUTTING INSTRUCTIONS

From white fabric, cut:

- ▶ (1) 4½" × 21" (11.5 cm × 53.5 cm) strip; subcut into (4) 4½" (11.5 cm) squares
- ▶ (1) 5¼" × 21" (13.5 cm × 53.5 cm) strip; subcut (2) 5¼" (13.5 cm) squares; cut the squares diagonally twice to create 8 quarter-square triangles

From red fabric, cut:

- ▶ (1) 4½" × 21" (11.5 cm × 53.5 cm) strip; subcut (1) 4½" (11.5 cm) square
- ▶ (1) 5¼" × 21" (13.5 cm × 53.5 cm) strip; subcut (2) 5¼" (13.5 cm) squares; cut diagonally twice to create 8 quarter-square triangles

BLOCK ASSEMBLY

1. Referring to FIGURE 1, sew together 1 white and 1 red quarter-square triangle to form half of the Quarter-Square unit. Trim dog-ears and press seams open. Make 8 units.

2. Sew 2 halves together to make a full Quarter-Square unit. Press seams open. Blocks should measure 4½" (11.5 cm) square (FIGURE 2). Make 4 units.

3. Lay out the rows as shown (FIGURE 3), being sure not to join like colors:

▸ **ROWS 1 AND 3:** (1) 4½" (11.5 cm) white square, 1 Quarter-Square unit, (1) 4½" (11.5 cm) white square

▸ **ROW 2:** 1 Quarter-Square unit, (1) 4½" (11.5 cm) red square, 1 Quarter-Square unit

▸ Sew the rows together (FIGURE 4). Press the seams open.

4. Square up the block to 12½" (31.5 cm) square. Once sewn in a quilt, the finished size is 12" (30.5 cm) square.

FIGURE 1

FIGURE 2

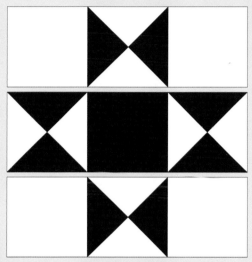

FIGURE 3

FIGURE 4

Ohio Star
Circa 1991
Maker Unknown
39½" × 71"
(100.5 cm × 180.5 cm)

Our Village Green

TECHNIQUE: Piecing   FINISHED SIZE: 12" (30.5 cm) square

The block name seems fitting for a design that has a large open center surrounded by half-squares.

MATERIALS

- ☐ White fabric, 1 fat eighth (9" × 21" [23 cm × 53.5 cm])
- ☐ Red fabric, 1 fat quarter (18" × 21" [45.5 cm × 53.5 cm])
- ☐ Red and white thread

CUTTING INSTRUCTIONS

From white fabric, cut:

▸ (2) 3⅜" × 21" (8.5 cm × 53.5 cm); subcut (6) 3⅜" (8.5 cm) squares; subcut each square diagonally twice to make 24 quarter-square triangles

From red fabric, cut:

▸ (1) 6½" (16.5 cm) square

▸ (2) 3⅜" × 21" (7.6 cm) strips; subcut (6) 3⅜" (8.6cm) squares; subcut each square diagonally twice into 24 quarter-square triangles

BLOCK ASSEMBLY

1. Sew 1 red quarter-square triangle and 1 white quarter-square triangle together to make a Square Triangle unit (FIGURE 1). Trim dogears and press the seams open. Make 12 units. Units should measure 2⅝" (6.5 cm) square

2. Join 2 white triangles, 2 red triangles, and 2 Square Triangle units as shown to create Corner unit A (FIGURE 2). Press the seams open. Make 2 units.

3. Join 2 white triangles, 2 red triangles, and 2 Square Triangle units as shown to create Corner unit B (FIGURE 3). Press the seams open. Make 2 units.

4. Sew 2 white triangles to adjoining sides of a red side of a Half-Square Triangle unit as shown to create Center unit A (FIGURE 4). Make 2 units. Press the seams open.

TIME-SAVER TIP

The following fabric cutting dies can make the cutting process faster and more accurate:

- ■ For 3" (7.5 cm) squares, use GO! Square #55256 3" (7.5 cm) [Finished 2½" (6.5 cm)]
- ■ For 6½" (16.5 cm) squares, use GO! Square #55000 6½" (16.5 cm) [Finished 6" (15 cm)]

5. Sew 2 red triangles to adjoining sides of a white side of a Quarter-Square Triangle unit as shown to make Corner unit B (FIGURE 5). Make 2 units. Press the seam open.

6. Referring to FIGURE 6, sew the 4 Center units to the 6½" (16.5 cm) red square as shown. Then join the 4 Corner units. Press the seams open.

7. Square up the block to 12½" (31.5 cm) square. Once sewn in a quilt, the finished size is 12" (30.5 cm) square.

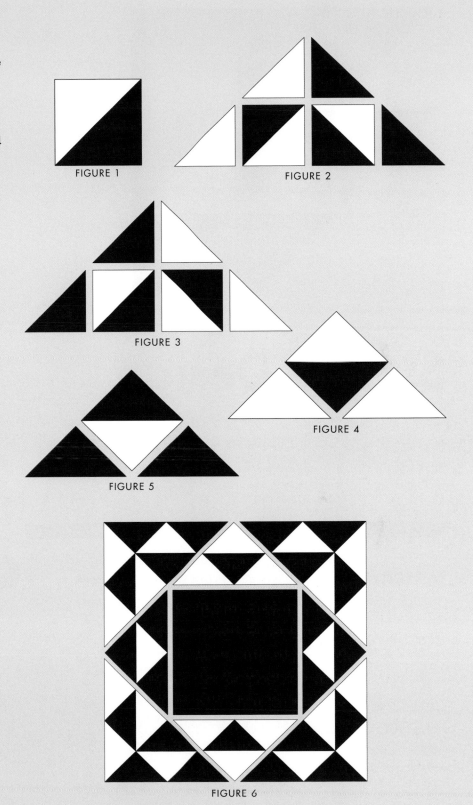

FIGURE 1

FIGURE 2

FIGURE 3

FIGURE 4

FIGURE 5

FIGURE 6

Simple Design

TECHNIQUE: Piecing   FINISHED SIZE: 12" (30.5 cm) square

Also known as Corn and Beans and North Wind, this block uses two different sizes of half-square triangles to create a wonderful diagonal pattern.

MATERIALS
- ☐ White fabric, 1 fat quarter (18" × 21" [45.5 cm × 53.5 cm])
- ☐ Red fabric, 1 fat quarter (18" × 21" [45.5 cm × 53.5 cm])
- ☐ Red and white thread

CUTTING INSTRUCTIONS

NOTE: *You will have 1 leftover of each of the large half-square triangles and each of the smaller half-square triangles.*

From white fabric, cut:
- ▸ (1) 8⅞" (22.5 cm) square; subcut diagonally into 2 half-square triangles
- ▸ (3) 4⅞" (12.5 cm) squares; subcut diagonally into 6 half-square triangles

From red fabric, cut:
- ▸ (1) 8⅞" (22.5 cm) square; subcut diagonally into 2 half-square triangles
- ▸ (3) 4⅞" (12.5 cm) squares; subcut diagonally into 6 half-square triangles

BLOCK ASSEMBLY

1. Join (1) 4⅞" (12.5 cm) red half-square triangle and (1) 4⅞" (12.5 cm) white half-square triangle to make a Half-Square Triangle unit (FIGURE 1). Trim dog ears and press seams open. Make 3 units. Half-Square Triangle units should measure 4½" (11.5 cm) square.

2. Referring to FIGURE 2, make the Center unit:

- ▸ Sew (1) 4⅞" (12.5 cm) red half-square triangle to the bottom of the white side of a Half-Square Triangle unit.

- ▸ Sew (1) 4⅞" (12.5 cm) white half-square triangle to the top of the red part of a Half-Square Triangle unit. Then sew (1) 4⅞" (12.5 cm) red half-square triangle to the bottom of that same unit.

- ▸ Sew (1) 4⅞" (12.5 cm) white half-square triangle to the top of the red part of a Half-Square Triangle unit.

- ▸ Sew the 3 pieces together as shown. Press seams open.

TIME-SAVER TIP

The following fabric cutting die can make the cutting process faster and more accurate:

- ■ For 4½" (11.5 cm) half-squares triangles, use GO! Half Square Triangle #55031 [Finished 4" (10 cm)]

- ■ For 8½" (21.5 cm) half-square triangles, use GO! Half Square Triangle #55400 [Finished 8" (20.5 cm)]

3. Referring to FIGURE 3, sew (1) 8⅞" (22.5 cm) white half-square triangle and (1) 8⅞" (22.5 cm) red half-square triangle on opposite sides of the Center unit to complete the block (FIGURE 4). Press seams open.

4. Using a rotary cutter and 12½" (31.5 cm) square ruler, trim the block to 12½" (31.5 cm) square. Once sewn in a quilt, the finished size is 12" (30.5 cm) square.

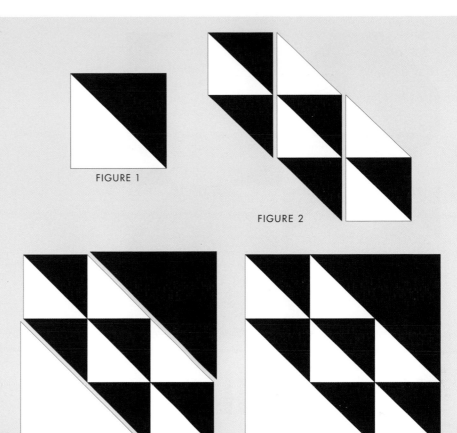

FIGURE 1

FIGURE 2

FIGURE 3

FIGURE 4

The Simply Touching Stars Quilt features a repeating pattern of Simple Design blocks.

Snowball

TECHNIQUE: Piecing   FINISHED SIZE: 12" (30.5 cm) square

The Snowball block is one that fools the eye. It can appear as having a rounded shape from a distance, but they are actually octagons.

MATERIALS

- ☐ White fabric, 1 fat quarter (18" × 21" [45.5 cm × 53.5 cm])
- ☐ Red fabric, 1 fat quarter (18" × 21" [45.5 cm × 53.5 cm])
- ☐ Red and white thread

CUTTING INSTRUCTIONS

From white fabric, cut:

- ▸ (1) 6½" (16.5 cm) × WOF (width-of-fabric) strip; subcut (2) 6½" (16.5 cm) squares
- ▸ (1) 2½" (6.5 cm) × WOF strip; subcut (8) 2½" (6.5 cm) squares

From red fabric, cut:

- ▸ (1) 6½" (16.5 cm) × WOF strips; subcut (2) 6½" (16.5 cm) squares.
- ▸ (1) 2½" (6.5 cm) × WOF strip; subcut (8) 2½" (6.5 cm) squares

BLOCK ASSEMBLY

1. Using a fabric pencil, lightly draw a diagonal line from corner to corner on each 2½" (6.5 cm) square. This will be your stitch line.

2. Lay (1) 2½" (6.5 cm) red square in each corner of the 6½" (16.5 cm) white square with edges aligned and pencil marks facing up (FIGURE 1). Sew along the stitch lines, then trim to ¼" (6 mm) seam allowance (FIGURE 2). Press the square to form the corner, then press the seam open to prevent shadowing (FIGURE 3). Sew 2 Red Snowball units.

3. Referring to FIGURE 4, lay (1) 2½" (6.5 cm) white square in each corner of the 6½" (16.5 cm) red square with edges aligned and pencil mark facing up. Sew along the stitch line, then trim to ¼" (6 mm) seam allowance and press square to form corner. Then press the seam open to prevent shadowing. Sew 2 White Snowball units.

4. Referring to FIGURE 5, sew 1 Red and 1 White Snowball units together. Repeat for the second pair. Press the seams open. Then sew the 2 rows together, alternating the positions of the red and white blocks (FIGURE 6). Press the seams open.

5. Square up the block to 12½" (31.5 cm) square. Once sewn in a quilt, the finished size is 12" (30.5 cm) square.

TIME-SAVER TIP

The following fabric cutting dies can make the cutting process faster and more accurate:

- ■ For 2½" (6.5 cm) squares, use GO! Value Die #55018
- ■ For 6½" (16.5 cm) squares, use GO! Square 55000 6½" (16.5 cm) [Finished 6" (15 cm)]

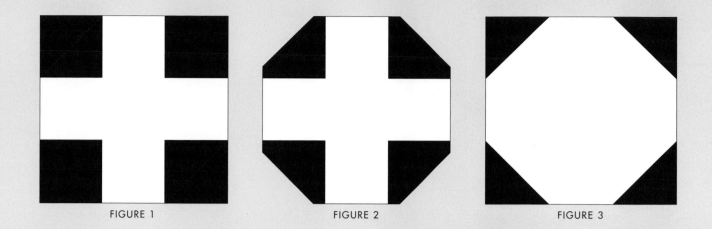

FIGURE 1   FIGURE 2   FIGURE 3

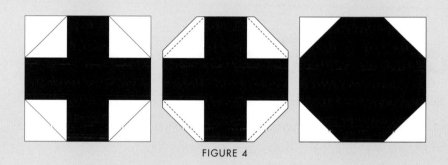

FIGURE 4

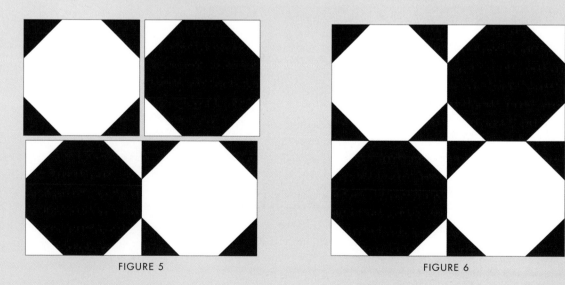

FIGURE 5   FIGURE 6

BLOCK ASSEMBLY

1. Sew together 1 red quarter-square triangle and 1 white quarter-square triangle to make a Half-Square Triangle unit (FIGURE 1). Trim dog-ears and press seams open. Trimmed Half-Square Triangle units should measure 3⅜" (8.5 cm). Make 12 Half-Square Triangle units.

2. Referring to FIGURE 2, lay out each diagonal row as shown. Place each 2⅞" (7.5 cm) half-square triangle in a corner. Sew the blocks together in diagonal rows. Then sew the rows together (FIGURE 3). Press seams open.

3. Square up the block to 12½" (31.5 cm) square. Once sewn in a quilt, the finished size will be 12" (30.5 cm) square.

Unnamed Block

TECHNIQUE: Piecing   FINISHED SIZE: 12" (30.5 cm) square

It is sad that this block made from half-squares has remained unnamed. The rectangle that forms in the center is unusual and creates interest.

MATERIALS

☐ White fabric, 1 fat quarter (18" × 21" [45.5 cm × 53.5 cm])

☐ Red fabric, 1 fat quarter (18" × 21" [45.5 cm × 53.5 cm])

☐ Red and white thread

CUTTING INSTRUCTIONS

From white fabric, cut:

▸ (3) 3¾" × 22" (9.5 cm × 56 cm) strips; subcut (6) 3¾" (9.5 cm) squares; subcut each square diagonally into 12 half-square triangles for side-setting triangles

▸ (1) 4⅛" (10.5 cm) × WOF (width-of-fabric) strip; subcut (2) 4⅛" (10.5 cm) squares, then subcut squares diagonally twice to make 8 quarter-squares; subcut (2) 2⅞" (7.5 cm) squares, then subcut squares diagonally to make 4 half-square triangles for corners

From red fabric, cut:

▸ (3) 3¾" × 22" (9.5 cm × 56 cm) strips; subcut (6) 3¾" (9.5 cm) squares; subcut squares diagonally to make 12 half-square triangles

▸ (1) 3⅜" (8.5 cm) square

▸ (1) 4⅛" × 22" (10.5 cm × 56 cm) strip; subcut (2) 4⅛" (10.5 cm) squares; subcut diagonally twice into 8 quarter-square triangles

FIGURE 1

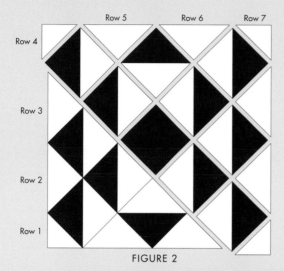

Row 4

Row 5 Row 6 Row 7

Row 3

Row 2

Row 1

FIGURE 2

FIGURE 3

Unnamed Blocks frame the center square in the Our Village Green Wall Hanging.

Wild Goose Chase

TECHNIQUE: Piecing   FINISHED SIZE: 12" (30.5 cm) square

When you're on a wild goose chase, it means you're pursuing an uncertain path that is doomed for failure. When making this block, however, if you cut carefully, sew accurately, and press neatly, you are bound to find success. In fact, this block may even become a favorite.

BLOCK ASSEMBLY

Refer to FIGURE 1 for steps 1–2.

1. Sew (1) 2⅝" (6.5 cm) white half-square triangle to each short side of (1) 3¼" (8.5 cm) red half-square triangle to form Flying Geese units. Trim dog-ears and press seams open. The unit should measure 2" × 3⅞" (5 cm × 10 cm). Make 12 Flying Geese units.

2. Sew 3 Flying Geese units together as shown. Make 4 sets.

3. Sew (1) 3¼" (8.5 cm) white half-square triangle to the bottom of each Flying Geese unit (FIGURE 2). Trim dog-ears and press seam open.

4. Sew 1 Flying Geese unit on opposite sides of the 3⅞" (10 cm) square to complete the center row (FIGURE 3). Press the seams open.

5. Sew (1) 8⅜" (21.5 cm) white triangle to each side of a Flying Geese unit to form a Corner unit. Press the seams open. Make 2 Corner units (FIGURE 4).

MATERIALS

☐ White fabric, 1 fat quarter (18" × 21" [45.5 cm × 53.5 cm])

☐ Red fabric, 1 fat eighth (9" × 21" [23 cm × 53.5 cm])

☐ Red and white thread

CUTTING INSTRUCTIONS

From white fabric, cut:

▸ (2) 2⅝" × 21" (6.5 cm × 53.5 cm) strips; subcut into (12) 2⅝" (6.5 cm) squares; subcut squares diagonally to make 24 half-square triangles for Flying Geese unit backgrounds

▸ (1) 3" × 21" (7.5 cm × 53.5 cm) strip; subcut into (2) 3" (7.5 cm) squares; subcut squares diagonally to make 4 half-square triangles for the block corners

▸ (1) 8⅜" (21.5 cm) square; subcut diagonally twice to make 4 quarter-square triangles for block sides

From red fabric, cut:

▸ (2) 3" × 21" (7.5 cm × 53.5 cm) strips; subcut into (6) 3" (7.5 cm) squares; subcut squares diagonally to make 12 half-square triangles for the Flying Geese units

▸ (1) 3⅞" (10 cm) square

6. Sew 1 Corner unit to each long side of the center row (FIGURE 5). Press seams open.

7. Square up the block to 12½" (31.5 cm) square. Once sewn in a quilt, the finished size will be 12" (30.5 cm) square.

FIGURE 1

FIGURE 2

FIGURE 3

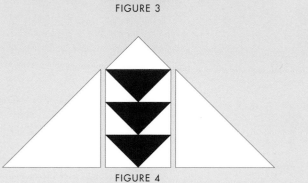

FIGURE 4

FIGURE 5

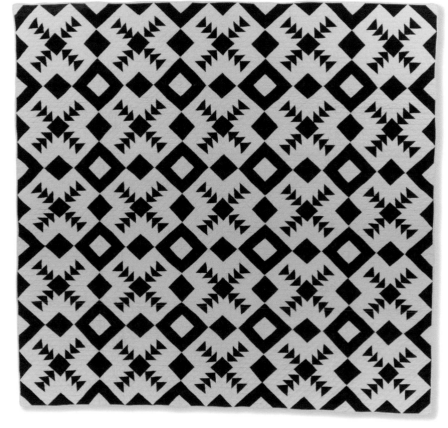

Wild Goose Chase
1880–1900
Maker Unknown
77½" × 78½"
(197 cm × 199.5 cm)

Handkerchief

TECHNIQUE: Appliqué   FINISHED SIZE: 16" (40.5 cm) square

Although historically used for personal hygiene, handkerchiefs were often highly decorated and beautiful. I can't help but wonder if this block was inspired by such an everyday item.

BLOCK ASSEMBLY

Refer to FIGURE 1 throughout assembly.

1. Locate the center of the white square by folding the fabric horizontally, vertically, and diagonally in both directions and creasing lightly (see Finding the Center of a Block in chapter 1).

2. Press part E in the center of the background square.

3. Press part A in the center of part E.

4. Center and press 1 part D on each horizontal fold line 1" (2.5 cm) from the edge of part A as shown.

5. Center and press 1 part C on each diagonal fold line ½" (1.3 cm) from the edge of a part D.

6. Press 1 Part B on each diagonal line ⅜" (1 cm) from the edge of part E.

MATERIALS

☐ White fabric, (1) fat quarter (18" × 21" [45.5 cm × 53.5 cm])

☐ Red fabric, 1 fat quarter (18" × 21" [45.5 cm × 53.5 cm])

☐ Paper-backed fusible web, ½ yard (0.5 m)

☐ Lightweight fusible interfacing, ½ yard (0.5 m)

☐ Red and white thread

☐ Handkerchief templates (on CD)

CUTTING INSTRUCTIONS

Follow manufacturer's directions for fusing the paper-backed fusible web to the "pre-fused" fabric before cutting fabric.

From white fabric, cut:

▸ (1) 18" (45.5 cm) square

From "pre-fused" white fabric, cut:

NOTE: *To prevent shadowing through of the red background, line white fabric with lightweight interfacing.*

▸ 1 part A
▸ 4 part B
▸ 4 part C
▸ 4 part D

From "pre-fused" red fabric, cut:

▸ 1 part E

7. Appliqué the shapes with your favorite stitch using white thread for parts A–D and red thread for part E.

8. Using a rotary cutter and 6" × 24" (15 cm × 61 cm) quilt ruler, trim the block to 16½" (42 cm) square. Once sewn in a quilt, the finished size is 16" (40.5 cm) square.

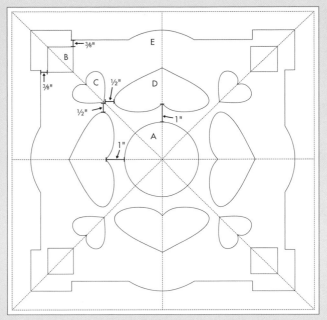

FIGURE 1

The Heart Handkerchief Quilt showcases this beautiful block with white designs on red fabric.

Oak Leaf and Flower

TECHNIQUE: Appliqué   FINISHED SIZE: 16" (40.5 cm) square

Legend has it the oak tree was the most powerful tree. It is used as a symbol of balance, purpose, and strength. In Greek and Roman lore it is associated with the gods Zeus and Jupiter. Even today the military uses an oak leaf to represent leadership. It is no wonder the oak leaf has been a popular quilting motif since the nineteenth century.

BLOCK ASSEMBLY

Refer to FIGURE 1 throughout assembly.

FIGURE 1

1. Locate the center of the white square by folding the fabric horizontally, vertically, and diagonally in both directions and creasing lightly (see Finding the Center of a Block in chapter 1).

2. Press part C in the center of the block as shown.

3. Press part B on the horizontal and vertical lines and part A on the diagonal lines touching the edges of part C.

4. Appliqué the shapes with your favorite stitch using red thread.

5. Using a rotary cutter and 6" × 24" (15 cm × 61 cm) quilt ruler, trim the block to 16½" (42 cm) square. Once sewn in a quilt, the finished size is 16" (40.5 cm) square.

MATERIALS

- ☐ White fabric, 1 fat quarter (18" × 21" [45.5 cm × 53.5 cm])
- ☐ Red fabric, 1 fat quarter (18" × 21" [45.5 cm × 53.5 cm])
- ☐ Paper-backed fusible web, ½ yard (0.5 m)
- ☐ Red thread
- ☐ Oak Leaf and Flower templates (on CD)

CUTTING INSTRUCTIONS

Follow manufacturer's instructions for fusing the paper-backed fusible web to the "pre-fused" red fabric before cutting fabric.

From white fabric, cut:
- ▶ (1) 16½" (42 cm) square

From "pre-fused" red fabric, cut:
- ▶ 4 part A
- ▶ 4 part B
- ▶ 1 part C

BLOCK ASSEMBLY

Refer to FIGURE 1 throughout assembly.

FIGURE 1

1. Locate the center of the white square by folding the fabric horizontally, vertically, and diagonally in both the shapes directions and creasing lightly (see Finding the Center of a block in chapter 1).

2. Press part A in the center of the block.

NOTE: *To find the center of part A, fold the square in half lengthwise and horizontally.*

3. Arrange part B around part A. Then position 1 part C on each horizontal and vertical line and 1 part D on each diagonal line with the stems ⅛" (3 mm) under part B. Press the parts in place.

4. Appliqué with your favorite stitch using red thread.

5. Using a rotary cutter and 6" × 24" (15 cm × 61 cm) quilt ruler, trim the block to 16½" (42 cm) square. Once sewn in a quilt, the finished size is 16" (40.5 cm) square.

Oak Reel Version Two

TECHNIQUE: Appliqué   FINISHED SIZE: 16" (40.5 cm) square

Many variations of this popular nineteenth-century pattern have found their way into red and white quilts.

MATERIALS

- ☐ White fabric, 1 fat quarter (18" × 21" [45.5 cm × 53.5 cm])
- ☐ Red fabric, 1 fat quarter (18" × 21" [45.5 cm × 53.5 cm])
- ☐ Paper-backed fusible web, ¼ yard (0.2 m)
- ☐ Red thread
- ☐ Oak Reel Version Two templates (on CD)

CUTTING INSTRUCTIONS

Follow manufacturer's instructions for fusing the paper-backed fusible web to the "pre-fused" red fabric before cutting fabric.

From white fabric, cut:

- ▸ (1) 18" (45.5 cm) square

From "pre-fused" red fabric, cut:

- ▸ 1 part A
- ▸ 1 part B
- ▸ 4 part C
- ▸ 4 part D

Seven Sisters

TECHNIQUE: Appliqué   FINISHED SIZE: 16" (40.5 cm) square

According to legend, this design represents the seven Southern states that seceded from the Union before the inauguration of Abraham Lincoln on March 4, 1861.

MATERIALS

☐ White fabric, 1 fat quarter (18" × 21" [45.5 cm × 53.5 cm])

☐ Red fabric, 1 fat quarter (18" × 21" [45.5 cm × 53.5 cm])

☐ Paper-backed fusible web, ¼ yard (0.2 m)

☐ Red thread

☐ Seven Sisters template (on CD)

CUTTING INSTRUCTIONS

Follow manufacturer's directions for fusing the paper-backed fusible web to the "pre-fused" red fabric before cutting fabric.

From white fabric, cut:

▶ (1) 18" (45.5 cm) square

From "pre-fused" red fabric, cut:

▶ 7 part A

BLOCK ASSEMBLY

Refer to FIGURE 1 throughout assembly.

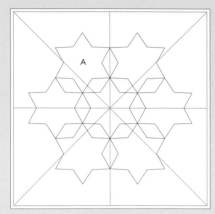

FIGURE 1

1. Locate the center of the white square by folding the fabric horizontally, vertically, and diagonally in both directions and creasing lightly (see Finding the Center of a Block in chapter 1).

2. Press 1 part A in the center of the background square. Press the remaining part A shapes in place, aligning the points of the stars as shown.

3. Appliqué with your favorite stitch using red thread.

4. Using a rotary cutter and 6" × 24" (15 cm × 61 cm) quilt ruler, trim the block to 16½" (42 cm) square. Once sewn in a quilt, the finished size is 16" (40.5 cm) square.

BLOCK ASSEMBLY

Refer to FIGURE 1 throughout assembly.

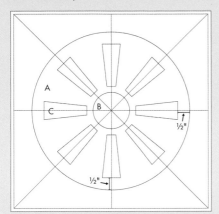

FIGURE 1

1. Locate the center of the white square by folding the fabric horizontally, vertically, and diagonally in both directions and creasing lightly (see Finding the Center in chapter 1).

2. Press part A in the center of the white square. Then press part B in the center of part A as shown.

3. Press 1 part C on each fold line ½" (1.3 cm) from the edge of part B as shown.

4. Appliqué with your favorite stitch, matching the thread color to your shapes.

5. Using a rotary cutter and 6" × 24" (15 cm × 61 cm) quilt ruler, trim the block to 16½" (42 cm) square. Once sewn in a quilt, the finished size is 16" (40.5 cm) square.

Wagon Wheel

TECHNIQUE: Appliqué   FINISHED SIZE: 16" (40.5 cm) square

This design brings to mind visions of covered wagons on the plains as the pioneers went West. Although visually dynamic, the block is actually quite simple and easy to appliqué.

MATERIALS

- ☐ White fabric, 1 fat quarter (18" × 21" [45.5 cm × 53.5 cm])
- ☐ Red fabric, 1 fat quarter (18" × 21" [45.5 cm × 53.5 cm])
- ☐ Paper-backed fusible web, ½" yard (0.5 m)
- ☐ Lightweight fusible interfacing, ⅛ yard (0.1 m)
- ☐ Red and white thread
- ☐ Wagon Wheel templates (on CD)

CUTTING INSTRUCTIONS

Follow manufacturer's directions for fusing the paper-backed fusible web to the "pre-fused" red and white fabric before cutting fabric. To prevent shadowing, line white fabric with lightweight fusible interfacing.

From white fabric, cut:

▸ (1) 18" (45.5 cm) square

From "pre-fused" white fabric, cut:

▸ 1 part B (3" [7.5 cm] circle)

▸ 8 part C

From "pre-fused" red fabric, cut:

▸ 1 part A (13" [33 cm] circle)

Drunkard's Path

TECHNIQUE: Piecing   FINISHED SIZE: 16" (40.5 cm) square

There are almost as many names for this block as there are ways to set it. Rob Peter to Pay Paul, Wanderer's Path in the Wilderness, Oregon Trail, Endless Trail, Solomon's Puzzle, and Fool's Puzzle, just to name a few. Using a red-and-white color combination for this block has been popular since the 1800s.

MATERIALS

- ☐ White fabric, ⅜ yard (0.4 m)
- ☐ Red fabric, ⅜ yard (0.4 m)
- ☐ Red and white thread

CUTTING INSTRUCTIONS

From white fabric, cut:

- ▸ 8 part A
- ▸ 8 part B

From red fabric, cut:

- ▸ 8 part A
- ▸ 8 part B

BLOCK ASSEMBLY

1. Sew together 1 white part A and 1 red part B (FIGURE 1). Press seam toward the red fabric. Make 8 units.

2. Sew together 1 red part A and 1 white part B (FIGURE 2). Press seam toward the red fabric. Make 8 units.

3. Referring to FIGURE 3, lay out the units in rows as shown. Sew the units together by row. Press the seams open. Sew the rows together (FIGURE 4). Press the seams open.

4. Square up the block to 16½" (42 cm) square. Once sewn in a quilt, the finished size is 16" (40.5 cm) square.

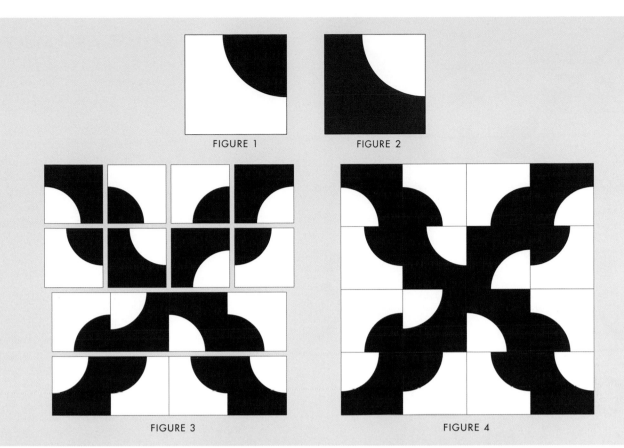

FIGURE 1   FIGURE 2

FIGURE 3   FIGURE 4

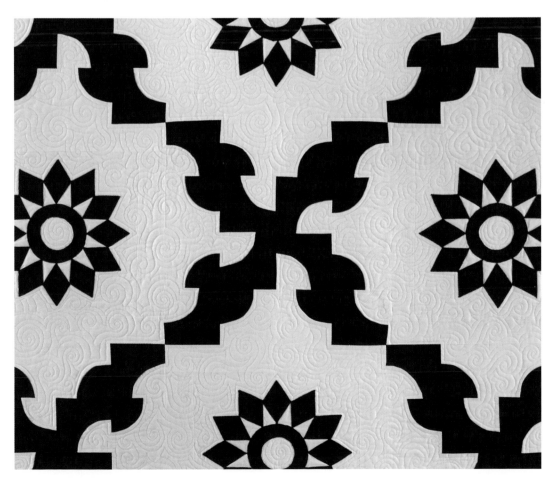

Drunkard's Path blocks appear to frame Sunburst blocks in the Drinking Party Quilt.

Oak Reel and Flowers

TECHNIQUE: Appliqué   FINISHED SIZE: 20" (51 cm) square

Spring has sprung on this beautiful block of tulips and five-petal flowers. The center motif is a version of the traditional Oak Reel design.

BLOCK ASSEMBLY

Refer to FIGURE 1 throughout assembly.

1. Locate the center of the white square by folding the fabric horizontally, vertically, and diagonally in both directions and creasing lightly (see Finding the Center in chapter 1).

2. Press part G in the center of the block. Align the points of each part F to the corners of part G and press.

3. Press each part A on a diagonal line 2" (5 cm) from the side of the block.

4. Arrange (1) ⅜" × 5¼" (1 cm × 13.5 cm) strip in each corner on the diagonal line for the flower stems. Place the ⅜" × 3¼" (1 cm × 8.5 cm) strips (the branches) about 2" (5 cm) from the side of the block and ⅛" (3 mm) under each ⅜" × 5¼" (1 cm × 13.5 cm) strip. Press into place.

5. Press (1) ⅜" × 3¼" (1 cm × 8.5 cm) strip on each horizontal and vertical line for the stems of the tulips.

MATERIALS

- ☐ White fabric, ⅝ yard (0.6 m)
- ☐ Red fabric, 1 fat quarter (18" × 21" [45.5 cm × 53.5 cm])
- ☐ Paper-backed fusible web, ½ yard (0.5 m)
- ☐ Red thread
- ☐ Oak Reel and Flowers templates (on CD)

CUTTING INSTRUCTIONS

Follow manufacturer's directions for fusing the paper-backed fusible web to the "pre-fused" red fabric before cutting fabric.

From white fabric, cut:

- ▸ (1) 22" (56 cm) square

From "pre-fused" red fabric, cut:

- ▸ 4 part A
- ▸ 12 part B
- ▸ 4 part C
- ▸ 24 part D
- ▸ 4 part E
- ▸ 4 part F
- ▸ 1 part G
- ▸ (3) ⅜" × 21" (1 cm × 53.5 cm) strips; subcut into (4) ⅜" × 5¼" (1 cm × 13.5 cm) strips and (12) ⅜" × 3¼" (1 cm × 8.5 cm) strips

6. Press parts E, B, and D (the leaves and flowers) in place as shown.

7. Appliqué with your favorite stitch using red thread.

8. Trim the block to 20½" (52 cm) square. Once sewn in a quilt, the finished size is 20" (51 cm) square.

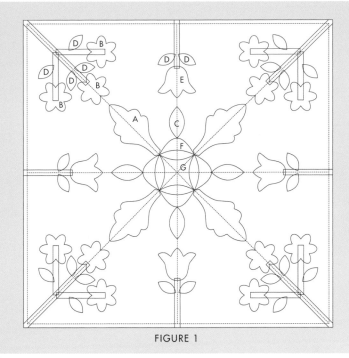

FIGURE 1

The Oak Reel and Flowers block features prominently in the Starry Flower Garden Quilt.

Paper Cut Appliqué

TECHNIQUE: Appliqué   FINISHED SIZE: 20" (51 cm) square

Intricate and outstanding, this design was inspired by the Paper Cut Appliqué quilt in the International Quilt Study Center & Museum's collection dating from 1852.

MATERIALS

- ☐ White fabric, ⅝ yard (0.4 m)
- ☐ Red fabric, 1 fat quarter (18" × 21" [46 cm × 53.5 cm])
- ☐ Paper-backed fusible web, ½ yard (0.5 m)
- ☐ Red thread
- ☐ Paper Cut templates (on CD)

CUTTING INSTRUCTIONS

Follow manufacturer's directions for fusing the paper-backed fusible web to the "pre-fused" red fabric before cutting fabric.

From white fabric, cut:

▸ (1) 22" (56 cm) square

From "pre-fused" red fabric, cut:

▸ 4 part A
▸ 4 part B
▸ 4 part C
▸ 1 part D

BLOCK ASSEMBLY

Refer to FIGURE 1 throughout assembly.

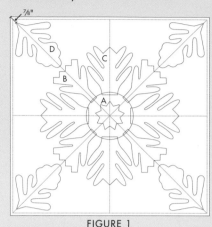

FIGURE 1

1. Locate the center of the white square by folding the fabric horizontally, vertically, and diagonally in both directions and creasing lightly (see Finding the Center in chapter 1).

2. Lay part A in the center of the white background square. Arrange each part B and part C around part A with ⅛" (3 mm) of the stems under circle. Press the pieces into place.

3. Press 1 part D on each diagonal line 1⅝" (4 cm) from the corner.

4. Appliqué with your favorite stitch using red thread.

5. Trim the block to 20½" (52 cm) square. Once sewn in a quilt, the finished size is 20" (51 cm) square.

BLOCK ASSEMBLY

Refer to FIGURE 1 throughout assembly.

FIGURE 1

1. Locate the center of the white square by folding the fabric horizontally, vertically, and diagonally in both directions and creasing lightly (see Finding the Center of a Block in chapter 1).

2. Lay part A in the center of the block.

3. Position each part B and part C alternating around part A as shown with the bottom edge ⅛" (3 mm) under the circle. Press the parts in place.

4. Appliqué with your favorite stitch using red thread.

5. Trim the block to 30½" (77.5 cm) square. Once sewn in a quilt, the finished size is 30" (76 cm) square.

Princess Feather

TECHNIQUE: Appliqué   FINISHED SIZE: 30" (76 cm) square

The Princess Feather quilt design comes in many variations, but all contain the main characteristic of a large plume feather-like shape. Princess Feather quilts were popular in the mid-1880s. Some think the design motif was inspired by the plant of the same name, while others claim the shape was inspired by the large plume feathers on the hats worn by royalty.

MATERIALS

☐ White fabric, ⅞ yard (0.8 m)
☐ Red fabric, ½ yard (0.5 m)
☐ Paper-backed fusible web, 1 yard (0.9 m)
☐ Red thread
☐ Princess Flower templates (on CD)

CUTTING INSTRUCTIONS

Follow manufacturer's directions for fusing the paper-backed fusible web to the "pre-fused" red fabric before cutting fabric.

From white fabric, cut:

▸ (1) 32" (81.5 cm) square

From "pre-fused" red fabric, cut:

▸ 1 part A
▸ 8 part B
▸ 8 part C

Carpenter's Square

TECHNIQUE: Appliqué   FINISHED SIZE: 30" (76 cm) square

Right angles and straight lines define this striking block. The design is inspired by quilts in the International Quilt Study Center & Museum dating from the mid-1850s. It was named for a tool commonly used by carpenters to define angles and lay out squares during the time period when this block first appeared.

BLOCK ASSEMBLY

1. Locate the center of the white square by folding the fabric horizontally, vertically, and diagonally in both directions and creasing lightly (see Finding the Center of a Block in chapter 1).

2. With a fabric pencil, lightly draw a 4" (10 cm) square diagonally around the center point as shown (FIGURE 1). Then extend the diagonal lines on either side of the square going in both directions.

3. Press the ½" (1.3 cm) wide strips on the folded and drawn lines. Referring to FIGURE 2, press strips in sequence as shown, spacing strips ¾" (2 cm) apart. Trim strips at the block edge.

4. Appliqué with your favorite stitch using red thread.

5. Trim the block to 30½" (77.5 cm) square. Once sewn in a quilt, the finished size is 30" (76 cm) square.

MATERIALS

- ☐ White fabric, ⅞ yard (0.8 m)
- ☐ Red fabric, ⅓ yard (0.3 m)
- ☐ Paper-backed fusible web, ½ yard (0.5 m)
- ☐ Red and white thread

CUTTING INSTRUCTIONS

Follow manufacturer's directions for fusing the paper-backed fusible web to the "pre-fused" red fabric before cutting fabric.

From white fabric, cut:

▸ (1) 32" (81.5 cm) square

From red "pre-fused" fabric, cut:

▸ (16) ½" (1.3 cm) × WOF (width-of-fabric) strips

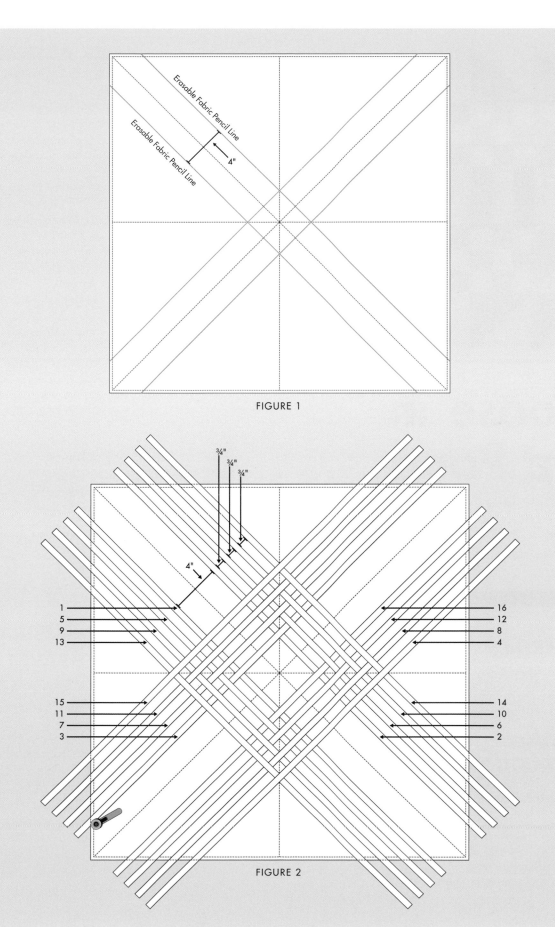

FIGURE 1

FIGURE 2

Goose in the Pond

TECHNIQUE: Piecing   FINISHED SIZE: 30" (76 cm) square

This oversized Five-Patch block gives a simple, traditional design a contemporary feel.

MATERIALS

☐ White fabric, ¾ yard (0.7 m)
☐ Red fabric, ¾ yard (0.7 m)
☐ Red and white thread

CUTTING INSTRUCTIONS

From white fabric, cut:

▶ (2) 6⅞" (17.5cm) × WOF (width-of-fabric) strips; subcut (6) 6⅞" (17.5 cm) squares, then cut each square diagonally into 2 half-square triangles

▶ (3) 2½" (6.5cm) × WOF strips

▶ (1) 6½" (16.5cm) × WOF strip; subcut into (5) 6½" (16.5 cm) squares

From red fabric, cut:

▶ (2) 6⅞" (17.5cm) × WOF strips; subcut (6) 6⅞" (17.5 cm) squares, then cut each square diagonally into 2 half-square triangles

▶ (3) 2½" (6.5 cm) × WOF strips

▶ (1) 6½" (16.5 cm) × WOF strip; subcut into (5) 6½" (16.5 cm) squares

BLOCK ASSEMBLY

1. Sew together 1 red and 1 white Half-Square Triangle unit (FIGURE 1). Trim dog-ears and press seams open. Unit should measure 6½" (16.5 cm) square. Make 12 Half-Square Triangle units.

2. Make strip set 1 by sewing together (3) 2½" (6.5 cm) × WOF strips in this order 1 red, 1 white, and 1 red. Press the seams open. From the strip set, cut (4) 6½" (16.5 cm) squares. From the remaining strip, cut (4) 2½" × 6½" (6.5 cm × 16.5 cm) strips (FIGURE 2).

3. Make strip set 2 by sewing together (3) 2½" (6.5 cm) × WOF strips in this order 1 white, 1 red, and 1 white. Press the seams open. Cut the strip set into (8) 2½" × 6½" (6.5 cm × 16.5 cm) strips (FIGURE 3).

4. Sew strips together in this order 1 white/red/white, 1 red/white/red, and 1 white/red/white as shown (FIGURE 4). Press the seams open. Make 4 Nine Patch units.

5. Referring to FIGURE 5, arrange the rows as follows:

▸ **ROWS 1 AND 5:** (2) 6½" (16.5 cm) Half-Square units, (1) 6½" (16.5 cm) white square, and (2) 6½" (16.5 cm) Half-Square Triangle units. Position Half-Square Triangle units facing the center of the block.

▸ **ROWS 2 AND 4:** (1) 6½" (16.5 cm) Half-Square Triangle unit, 1 Nine Patch unit, (1) 6½" (16.5 cm) square strip set unit placed horizontally, 1 Nine Patch unit, and (1) 6½" (16.5 cm) Half-Square Triangle unit. Position all Triangle units facing the center of the block.

▸ **ROW 3:** (3) 6½" (16.5 cm) white squares and (2) 6½" (16.5 cm) Square Strip Set units placed vertically, starting with a white square and alternating the units.

Sew the units together by row. Press the seams open.

6. Sew the rows together (FIGURE 6). Press the seams open. The block should measure 30½" (77.5 cm) square. Once sewn in a quilt, the finished size is 30" (76 cm) square.

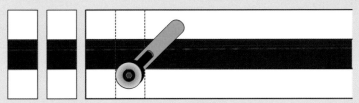

FIGURE 1

FIGURE 2: STRIP SET 1

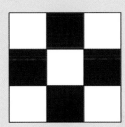

FIGURE 3: STRIP SET 2

FIGURE 4

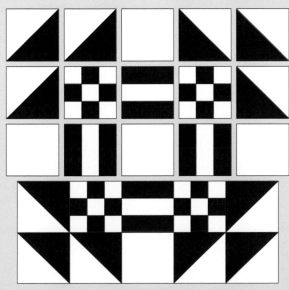

FIGURE 5

FIGURE 6

Sawtooth Square

TECHNIQUE: Piecing   FINISHED SIZE: 30" (76 cm) square

Basic Half-Square and Quarter-Square units make up this high-impact design. The large block could be a wall-hanging on its own, but it also work well when combined with other blocks or used in a border.

MATERIALS

☐ White fabric, 1 yard (0.9 m)
☐ Red fabric, 1 yard (0.9 m)
☐ Red and white thread

CUTTING INSTRUCTIONS

From white fabric, cut:

▸ (3) 2⅝" (6.5 cm) × WOF (width-of-fabric) strips; subcut (30) 2⅝" (6.5 cm) squares, then cut diagonally into 60 half-square triangles

▸ (2) 7⅛" (18 cm) squares; subcut diagonally into 4 half-square triangles

▸ (2) 15⅞" (40.5 cm) squares; subcut diagonally into 4 half-square triangles

From red fabric, cut:

▸ (1) 5¾" (14.5 cm) square

▸ (2) 2⅝" (6.5 cm) × WOF strip; subcut (30) 2⅝" (6.5 cm) squares, then cut diagonally into 60 half-square triangles

▸ (2) 9⅝" (24.5 cm) squares; subcut diagonally into 4 half-squares triangles

BLOCK ASSEMBLY

Note the orientation of the blocks when sewing together the strip sets.

1. Sew together 1 red and 1 white 2⅝" (6.5 cm) half-square triangle (FIGURE 1). Make 60 Half-Square Triangle units. Trim dog-ears and press seams open. Units should measure 2¼" (5.5 cm) square. Press seams open.

2. Make strip set 1 by sewing together (3) 2¼" (5.5 cm) Half-Square Triangle units as shown (FIGURE 2). Make 2 sets. Press seams to red side of seam.

3. Make strip set 2 by sewing together (5) 2¼" (5.5 cm) Half-Square Triangle units as shown (FIGURE 3), noting the orientation of the blocks. Make 2 sets. Press seams to red side of seam.

4. Referring to FIGURE 4, sew strip set 1 to opposite sides of the 5¾" (14.5 cm) red square. Sew strip set 2 to the remaining sides. Press seams open. Sew (1) 7⅛" (18 cm) white half-square triangle to each side of the Center unit. Press seams open.

5. Sew (1) 9⅝" (24.5 cm) red half-square triangle to each side of the center unit (FIGURE 5). Press seams to red side of seam.

6. Make strip set 3 by sewing together (10) 2¼" (5.5 cm) Half-Square Triangle units as shown (FIGURE 6). Make 2 sets. Press seams to red side of seam.

7. Make strip set 4 by sewing together (12) 2¼" (5.5 cm) Half-Square units as shown (FIGURE 7). Make 2 sets. Press seams to red side of seam.

8. Referring to FIGURE 8, sew strip set 3 to opposite sides of the Center unit. Sew strip set 4 to the remaining sides. Then sew (4) 15⅞" (40.5 cm) white half-square triangles to the block. Press the seams open. The block should measure 30½" (77.5 cm) square. Once sewn in a quilt, the finished size is 30" (76 cm) square.

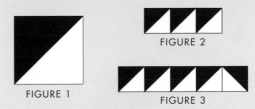

FIGURE 1

FIGURE 2

FIGURE 3

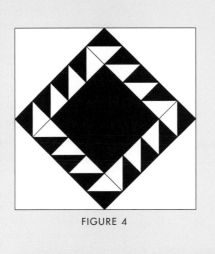

FIGURE 4

FIGURE 5

FIGURE 6

FIGURE 7

FIGURE 8

Touching Stars

TECHNIQUE: Piecing   FINISHED SIZE: 48" (122 cm) square

Quilts made of four large blocks were popular from the 1850s through the early 1900s. Similar to a Lone Star block, Touching Stars is stunning in a contrast of red and white fabric. Switch out the corner squares with a pieced block to add additional interest to the design.

MATERIALS

☐ White fabric, 2⅝ yards (2.4 m)

☐ Red fabric, 1 yard (0.9 m)

☐ Red and white thread

CUTTING INSTRUCTIONS

From white fabric, cut:

▸ (10) 2½" (6.5 cm) × WOF (width-of-fabric) strips

▸ (4) 14½" (37 cm) squares for corners

▸ (2) 21¼" (54 cm) squares; subcut diagonally into 4 half-square triangles

From red fabric, cut:

▸ (10) 2½" (6.5 cm) × WOF strips

BLOCK ASSEMBLY

1. Arrange (5) 2½" (6.5 cm) strips in this order: 1 red, 1 white, 1 red, 1 white, and 1 red to make strip set 1. Offset the strips by 1" (2.5 cm) and sew together. Make 2 sets. Press seams open. Cut each strip set into (12) 2½" (6.5 cm) 45-degree diagonal strips (FIGURE 1). You will use 16 sets.

2. Arrange (5) 2½" (6.5 cm) wide strips in this order: 1 white, 1 red, 1 white, 1 red, and 1 white to make strip set 2. Offset the strips by 1" (2.5 cm) and sew together. Make 2 sets. Press seams open. Cut each strip set into (12) 2½" (6.5 cm) 45-degree diagonal strips (FIGURE 2). Cut 24 sets.

3. Sew (5) 45-degree diagonal strips together as shown (FIGURE 3). Trim dog-ears and press seams open. Make 8 Star Point units.

4. Sew 2 Star Point units together. Trim dog-ears and press seams open. Make 4 sets.

5. Sew Star Point unit sets together as shown (FIGURE 4). Press seams open.

6. Sew on the 14½" (37 cm) white corner squares. Then sew the 21¼" (54 cm) white half-square triangles in the middle of the points as shown (FIGURE 5). Press seams open. The block should measure 48½" (123 cm). Once sewn in a quilt, the finished size is 48" (122 cm) square.

NOTE: *For tips on joining seams, see Sewing Y-Seams in chapter 1.*

2½"

FIGURE 1

2½"

FIGURE 2

FIGURE 3

FIGURE 4

FIGURE 5

FIGURE 6

CHAPTER 3
QUILTS & PROJECTS

The projects in this chapter use the featured red and white blocks from chapter 2 and highlight how they interplay with each other to create an overall design. Sewing blocks to blocks without a sashing can allow a secondary design to appear. The quilts Winter Time and Our Village Green in this book are perfect examples.

HAVE FUN MAKING THE QUILTS AND PROJECTS.

There are variations shown for each quilt or project, with more options available simply by using different blocks of the same size. Have fun making the quilts and projects as suggested—or create a new design of your own.

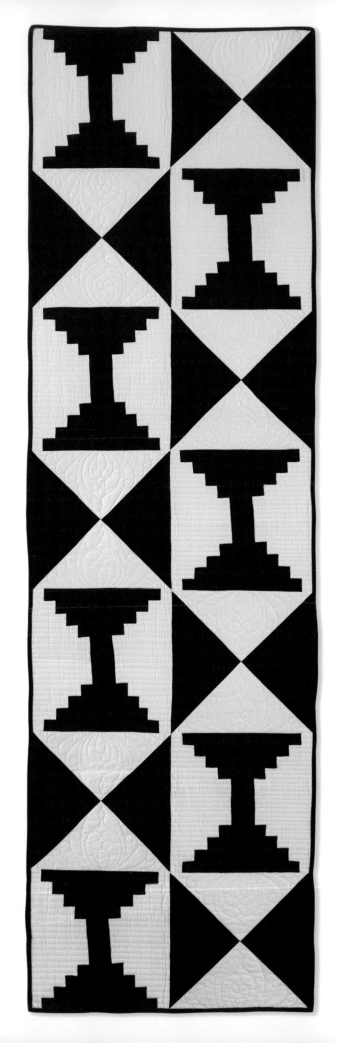

BALANCING ACT
BED RUNNER

PIECED BY **Lorna Pumphrey.** QUILTED BY **Karen Kielmeyer.**

FINISHED SIZE: 24" × 84"
(61 cm × 213.5 cm)

MATERIALS

Yardages are based on 40–42"
(101.5–106.5 cm) wide fabric.

- ☐ White fabric, 1⅞ yards
  (1.7 meters)
- ☐ Red fabric, 1⅜ yards (1.3 meters)
- ☐ Binding fabric, ⅝ yard (0.6 m)
- ☐ Backing fabric, 2½ yards (2.3 m)
- ☐ Twin–size quilt batting
- ☐ Thread for piecing

This simple graphic runner is made with a repeating pattern of two of the easier-to-piece 12" (30.5 cm) blocks, Courthouse Steps and the Hourglass. In literature, Courthouse Steps has been used to represent social equality, while the Hourglass has symbolized the need to rethink your thoughts and actions every once in a while, or always be drawn to one side. The symbolic meanings of these two blocks complement each other as does the appeal of their bold design.

CUTTING INSTRUCTIONS

Measurements include ¼" (6 mm) seam allowances. For best use of fabric, cut longer lengths from strips first.

From white fabric, cut:

☐ (3) 13¼" (33.5 cm) × WOF (width-of-fabric) strips; subcut into (7) 13¼" (33.5 cm) squares, cut squares diagonally twice into quarter-square triangles, leaving about a 13¼" × 26" (33.5 cm × 66 cm) strip

☐ Cut the 13¼" × 26" (33.5 cm × 66 cm) strip into (8) 1½" × 26" (3.8 cm × 66 cm) strips; subcut into (14) 1½" × 12½" (3.8 cm × 31.5 cm) logs, (14) 1½" × 10½" (3.8 cm × 26.7 cm) logs, and (14) 1½" × 2½" (3.8 cm × 6.5 cm) logs

☐ (7) 1½" (3.8 cm) × WOF strips; subcut into (14) 1½" × 8½" (3.8 cm × 21.5 cm) logs, (14) 1½" × 6½" (3.8 cm × 16.5 cm) logs, and (14) 1½" × 4½" (3.8 cm × 11.5 cm) logs

From red fabric, cut:

☐ (3) 13¼" (33.5 cm) × WOF strips; subcut into (7) 13¼" (33.5 cm) squares, then cut squares diagonally twice into quarter-square triangles, leaving about a 13¼" × 26" (66 cm) strip

☐ From the 13¼" × 26" (33.5 cm × 66 cm) strip, cut (8) 1½" × 26" (3.8 cm × 66 cm) strips; subcut into (14) 1½" × 10½" (3.8 cm × 26.7 cm) logs, (14) 1½" × 8½" (3.8 cm × 21.5 cm) logs, and (14) 1½" × 6½" (3.8 cm × 16.5 cm) logs

☐ (3) 1½" (3.8 cm) × WOF strips; subcut into (14) 1½" × 2½" (3.8 cm × 6.5 cm) logs and (14) 1½" × 4½" (3.8 cm × 11.5 cm) logs

☐ (1) 2½" (6.5 cm) × WOF strips; subcut into (7) 2½" (6.5 cm) squares

☐ (6) 2¼" (5.5 cm) × WOF strips for binding.

TIME-SAVER TIP

The following fabric cutting dies can make the cutting process faster and more accurate:

- For 2¼" (5.5 cm) bindings, use GO! Strip Cutter #55053 2¼" (5.5 cm) [Finished 1¾" (4.5 cm)]

- For 1½" (3.8 cm) for logs, use GO! Strip Cutter #55024 1½" (3.8 cm) [Finished 1" (2.5 cm)]

- For 2½" (6.5 cm) squares, use GO! Square #55059 2½" Multiples [Finished 2" (5 cm)]

VARIATIONS

You can use any of the 12" (30.5 cm) blocks in this setting, such as the Garden Maze and Crossroads blocks (VARIATION 1) or Basket and Small Basket blocks (VARIATION 2).

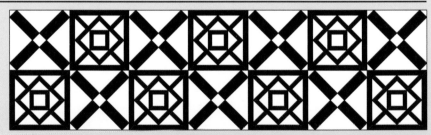

VARIATION 1

VARIATION 2

BLOCK ASSEMBLY

1. Following the instructions in chapter 2, make 7 Hourglass blocks (FIGURE 1) and 7 Courthouse Steps blocks (FIGURE 2).

BED RUNNER ASSEMBLY

2. Sew together 1 Hourglass block and 1 Courthouse Steps block (FIGURE 3). Press the seams open. Make 7 sets.

3. Pin and sew the sets together as shown. Press the seams open (FIGURE 4).

FINISHING THE BED RUNNER

4. Trim the backing to 30" × 90" (76 cm × 228.5 cm) and the batting to 32" × 94" (81.5 cm × 239 cm) wide.

5. Layer the backing (right-side down), batting, and quilt top (right-side up); baste. Quilt as desired. Square up the quilt, trimming away the extra batting and backing.

6. Join the 2¼" (5.5 cm) binding strips into one continuous piece for straight-grain French-fold binding (see French-Fold Binding in chapter 1). Add the binding to the quilt.

FIGURE 1

FIGURE 2

FIGURE 3

FIGURE 4

CARPENTER'S SQUARE QUILT

PIECED AND APPLIQUÉD BY **Linda Pumphrey.** MACHINE-QUILTED **by Karen Kielmeyer.**

FINISHED SIZE: 82"
(208.5 cm) square

MATERIALS

Yardages are based on 40–42"
(101.5–106.5 cm) wide fabric.

- ☐ White fabric, 4¾ yards (4.4 m)
- ☐ Red fabric, 7 yards (6.4 m)
- ☐ Backing fabric, 5 yards (4.6 m)
- ☐ Binding fabric, ⅞ yard (0.8 m)
- ☐ Queen-size quilt batting
- ☐ Paper-backed fusible web, 3½ yards (3.2 m)
- ☐ Thread for piecing

Carpenters use a steel square known as a Carpenter's Square to make perfect right angles. As in woodworking, precision is key when making Carpenter's Square blocks and this quilt. To give the traditional four-block design a more contemporary look, I placed the Carpenter's Square blocks on point and framed them with setting triangles. The result is dramatic and eye-catching.

CUTTING INSTRUCTIONS

Follow manufacturer's instructions for fusing the paper-backed fusible web to the red fabric before cutting fabric. Measurements include ¼" (6 mm) seam allowances.

From white fabric, cut:

☐ (5) 32" (81.5 cm) × WOF (width-of-fabric) strips; subcut into (5) 30½" (77.5 cm) squares

From red fabric, cut:

☐ (4) 43½" (110.5 cm) × WOF strips; subcut each strip into (4) 21¾" × 43½" (55 cm × 110.5 cm) rectangles, then find the middle point of each rectangle and cut a 45-degree line from the middle on each side as shown (FIGURE 1)

☐ (2) 22" (56 cm) × WOF strips; subcut into (2) 22" (56 cm) squares, then cut each square in half diagonally to form 4 half-squares for the corners

☐ (9) 2¼" (5.5 cm) × WOF strips for binding

From "pre-fused" red fabric, cut:

☐ (80) ½" (1.3cm) × WOF strips

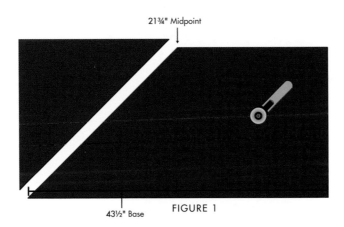

21¾" Midpoint

43½" Base

FIGURE 1

FIGURE 2

FIGURE 3

QUILT BLOCK ASSEMBLY

1. Following the Carpenter's Square block assembly instructions in chapter 2, make 5 blocks (FIGURE 2).

QUILT ASSEMBLY

2. Referring to FIGURE 3, lay out the quilt top as shown. You will need (4) 22" (56 cm) red corner half-squares, (4) 43½" (110.5 cm) red setting triangles, and 5 appliquéd Carpenter's Square blocks. Sew the rows together diagonally, then add the corners. Press the seams open.

FINISHING THE QUILT

3. Divide the backing into (2) 90" (228.5 cm) × WOF strips. Cut 1 piece in half lengthwise to make 2 narrower panels. Join 1 narrower panel to each side of the wider panel. Press the seams open.

4. Layer the backing (right-side down), batting, and quilt top (right-side up); baste. Quilt as desired. Square up the quilt, trimming away the extra batting and backing.

5. Join the 2¼" (5.5 cm) binding strips into one continuous piece for straight-grain French-fold binding (see French-Fold Binding in chapter 1). Add the binding to quilt.

VARIATIONS

You can use any of the 30" (76 cm) blocks in this fun and easy setting, such as the Princess Feather blocks (VARIATION 1) and Sawtooth Square blocks (VARIATION 2).

VARIATION 1

VARIATION 2

CHILDHOOD GAMES QUILT

PIECED BY **Linda Pumphrey.** MACHINE-QUILTED BY **Karen Kielmeyer.**

FINISHED SIZE: 94" (239 cm) square

MATERIALS

Yardages are based on 40–42" (101.5–106.5 cm) wide fabric. Border strips are exact length needed, so you may want to cut them longer to allow for piecing variations.

☐ White fabric, 2⅞ yards (2.6 m)

☐ Red fabric, 6 yards (5.5 m)

☐ Backing fabric, 8½ yards (7.8 m)

☐ Binding fabric, 1 yard (0.9 m)

☐ King-size quilt batting

☐ Thread for piecing

Just like in the poem "Snowball" by Shel Silverstein, you, too, can make a "snowball as perfect as it could be" and let it sleep with you. Snowballs bring visions of childhood memories of snowy winter days when snowball fights just happen. Combine it with another childhood memory of playing checkers on a cold winter evening by the fireplace to create this unique combination, a quilt full of fun memories and graphic appeal.

CUTTING INSTRUCTIONS

Measurements include ¼" (6 mm) seam allowances.

From white fabric, cut:

☐ (25) 2½" (6.5 cm) × WOF (width-of-fabric) strips; subcut into (2) 2½" × 36½" (6.5 cm × 92.5 cm) strips for the top and bottom inner white borders and (2) 2½" × 40½" (6.5 cm × 103 cm) strips for the inner side white borders; subcut (5) strips into (72) 2½" (6.5 cm) squares for Snowball blocks (the remaining 9 strips are for the Checkerboard block strip sets)

☐ (3) 6½" (16.5 cm) × WOF strips; subcut into (18) 6½" (16.5 cm) squares

From red fabric, cut:

☐ (2) 68½" (174 cm) × WOF lengthwise strips; subcut into (4) 12½" × 68½" (31.5 cm × 174 cm) strips for outer borders

☐ (2) 40½" (103 cm) × WOF lengthwise strips; subcut into (4) 12½" × 40½" (31.8 cm × 103 cm) rectangles for inner borders

From remaining red fabric, cut:

☐ (3) 6½" (16.5 cm) × WOF; subcut into (18) 6½" (16.5 cm) squares

☐ (16) 2½" (6.5 cm) × WOF strips; subcut (5) strips into (72) 2½" (6.5 cm) squares for Snowball blocks (the remaining 9 strips are for the Checkerboard block strip sets)

☐ (11) 2¼" (5.5 cm) × WOF strips for binding

QUILT BLOCK ASSEMBLY

1. Following the directions in chapter 2, make 9 Snowball blocks (FIGURE 1) and 8 Checkerboard blocks (FIGURE 2).

TIME-SAVER TIP

The following fabric cutting dies can make the cutting process faster and more accurate:

- For 2¼" (5.5 cm) bindings, use GO! Strip Cutter #55053 2¼" (5.5 cm) [Finished 1¾" (4.5 cm)]

- For 2½" (6.5 cm) strips, use GO! Strip Cutter #55017 2½" (6.5 cm) [Finished 2" (5 cm)]

- For 6½" (16.5 cm) squares, use GO! Square 55000 6½" (16.5 cm) [Finished 6" (15 cm)]

FIGURE 1

FIGURE 2

FIGURE 3

QUILT TOP CENTER ASSEMBLY

2. Referring to FIGURE 3, make Rows 1–3, noting the orientation of the blocks:

▸ **ROWS 1 AND 3:** Sew together in this order 1 Snowball block, 1 Checkerboard block, and 1 Snowball block. Press seams open.

▸ **ROW 2:** Sew together in this order 1 Checkerboard Block, 1 Snowball block and 1 Checkerboard block. Press seams open.

Sew the rows together along the long sides. Press seams open.

QUILT TOP ASSEMBLY

Refer to FIGURE 4 for steps 3–7.

3. Sew the 2½" × 36½" (6.5 cm × 92.5 cm) white inner borders to the top and bottom of the quilt center. Press seams open.

4. Sew the 2½" × 40½" (6.5 cm × 103 cm) white inner borders to the sides of the quilt center. Press seams open.

5. Sew the 12½" × 40½" (31.5 cm × 103 cm) red rectangles to top and bottom of quilt.

6. Sew 1 Snowball block to each short end of the remaining 12½" × 40½" (31.5 cm × 103 cm) red rectangles. Make 2 units.

7. Sew the Snowball units to each side of the quilt. Press the seams open.

BORDER ASSEMBLY

Refer to FIGURE 5 for steps 8–10.

8. Sew (2) 2½" (6.5 cm) × WOF white strips together. Press seams open. Make 4 strip sets. Trim 2 strip sets to 2½" × 64½" (6.5 cm × 164 cm), then sew 1 to the top and 1 to the bottom of the quilt. Press

seams open. Trim the remaining 2 strip sets to 2½" × 68½" (6.5 cm × 174 cm), then sew 1 to each side of the quilt. Press seams open.

9. Sew each 12½" × 68½" (31.5 cm × 174 cm) red outer border to the top and bottom of the quilt. Press seams open.

10. Sew a Checkerboard block to each short end of the remaining 12½" × 68½" (31.5 cm × 174 cm) red outer borders. Press seams open. Make 2 units.

11. Sew the red outer borders and the Checkerboard border units to the sides of the quilt. Press seams open.

FIGURE 4

FIGURE 5

FINISHING THE QUILT

12. Divide backing into (3) 102"
(2.6 m) × WOF lengths. Remove the
selvedges. Cut 1 piece in half lengthwise to make 2 narrower panels. Join
a narrower panel to one side of both
wider panels. Press seams open.

13. Layer the backing (right-side
down), batting, and quilt top (right-
side up); baste. Quilt as desired.

14. Join 2¼" (5.5 cm) binding
strips into one continuous piece for
straight-grain French fold binding (see
French-Fold Binding in Chapter 1).
Add the binding to the quilt.

VARIATIONS

You can use any combination of two
12" (30.5 cm) blocks to create a version of your own, such as the Ohio
Star and Five Quarter-Squares blocks
(VARIATION 1) or the Eight of Hearts
and Stars blocks (VARIATION 2).

VARIATION 1

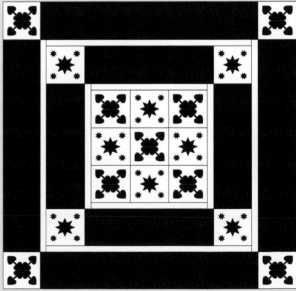

VARIATION 2

DRINKING PARTY QUILT

PIECED AND APPLIQUÉD BY **Linda Pumphrey**. MACHINE-QUILTED BY **Karen Kielmeyer**.

FINISHED SIZE: 84"
(213.5 cm) square

MATERIALS

Yardages are based on 40–42"
(101.5–106.5 cm) wide fabric. Border
strips are the exact length needed,
so you may want to cut them longer
to allow for piecing variations.

- ☐ White fabric, 7 yards (6.4 m)
- ☐ Red fabric, 4¾ yards (4.4 m)
- ☐ Backing fabric, 7⅔ yards (7 m)
- ☐ Binding fabric, ¾ yard (0.7 m)
- ☐ Queen-size quilt batting
- ☐ Paper-backed fusible
  web, 5 yards (4.6 m)
- ☐ Thread for piecing
- ☐ Thread for appliqué
- ☐ Drunkard's Path and Sunburst
  block templates (on CD)

At one time, quilters had a myth that if you slept under a
quilt made with Drunkard's Path blocks you would develop
a liking for drink just a little too much. In the Drinking Party
quilt, 16" (40.5 cm) Drunkard's Path blocks are used to create a pathway that highlights the alternating 12" (30.5 cm)
Sunburst blocks. This pattern uses 12" (30.5 cm) and 16"
(40.5 cm) blocks. By framing the 12" (30.5 cm) blocks, the
construction of this unusual quilt design becomes very simple.

CUTTING INSTRUCTIONS

Measurements include ¼" (6 mm) seam allowances.

From white fabric, cut:

☐ (20) 2½" (6.5 cm) × WOF strips; subcut into (24) 2½" × 12½" (6.5 cm × 31.5 cm) rectangles and (24) 2½" × 16½" (6.5 cm × 42 cm) rectangles for inner borders

☐ (4) 14" (35.5 cm) × WOF (width-of-fabric) strips; subcut into (12) 14" (35.5 cm) squares for Sunburst blocks

☐ 104 part A for Drunkard's Path blocks

☐ 104 part B for Drunkard's Path blocks

From red fabric, cut:

☐ 104 part A for Drunkard's Path blocks

☐ 104 part B for Drunkard's Path blocks

☐ (2) 2½" × 80½" (6.5 cm × 204.5 cm) rectangles for the top and borders

☐ (2) 2½" × 84½" (6.5 cm × 214.5 cm) for the side borders

☐ (9) 2¼" (5.5 cm) × WOF strips for the binding

NOTE: *Use the balance of the red fabric for the pre-fused fabric. Follow manufacturer's directions for fusing the paper-backed fusible web to the "pre-fused" red fabric before cutting fabric.*

From "pre-fused" red fabric, cut:

☐ 144 part A for Sunburst blocks

☐ 12 part B for Sunburst blocks

QUILT BLOCK ASSEMBLY

1. Following the instructions in chapter 1, make 13 Drunkard's Path blocks (FIGURE 1) and 12 Sunburst blocks (FIGURE 2).

2. Sew a 2½" × 12½" (6.5 cm × 31.5 cm) rectangle on each side of a Sunburst block. Press seams open. Then sew a 2½" × 16½" (6.5 cm × 42 cm) rectangle to the top and bottom of each Sunburst block. Press seams open. Repeat for each Sunburst block.

VARIATIONS

You can use any of the 12" (30.5 cm) and 16" (40.5 cm) blocks in this delightful design, such as the Checkerboard and Oak Reel Version Two blocks (VARIATION 1) or the Hourglass and Wagon Wheel blocks (VARIATION 2).

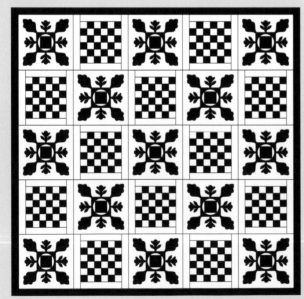

VARIATION 1

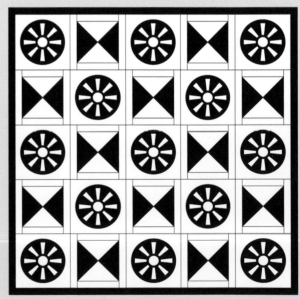

VARIATION 2

QUILT TOP ASSEMBLY

3. Sew a row with 1 Drunkard's Path block, 1 Sunburst block, 1 Drunkard's Path, 1 Sunburst block, and 1 Drunkard's Path block (FIGURE 3). Press seams open. Sew 3 row sets.

4. Sew a row with 1 Sunburst block, 1 Drunkard's Path block, 1 Sunburst block, 1 Drunkard's Path block, and 1 Sunburst block (FIGURE 4). Press seams open. Sew 2 row sets.

5. Referring to FIGURE 5, sew the rows together starting with row set 1. Join row set 2, then alternate the rows until all 5 rows are sewn together. Press seams open.

6. Sew a 2½" × 80½" (6.5 cm × 204.5 cm) red border to the top and bottom of the center panel. Then sew a 2½" × 84½" (6.5 cm × 214.6 cm) red border to each side. Press seams toward the red borders.

FINISHING THE QUILT

7. Divide backing into (3) 92" (233.5 cm) × WOF lengths and remove selvedges. Sew the 3 panels together along the long edges. Press seams open.

8. Layer backing (right-side down), batting, and quilt top (right-side up); baste. Quilt as desired.

9. Join the 2¼" (5.5 cm) binding strips into one continuous piece for straight-grain French-fold binding (see French-Fold Binding in chapter 1). Add the binding to the quilt.

FIGURE 1

FIGURE 2

FIGURE 3

FIGURE 4

FIGURE 5

DUCK, DUCK, GOOSE
WALL HANGING

PIECED BY **Mary Pumphrey.** MACHINE-QUILTED BY **Karen Kielmeyer.**

FINISHED SIZE: 42"
(106.5 cm) square

MATERIALS

Yardages are based on 40–42"
(101.5–106.5 cm) wide fabric. Border
strips are the exact length needed,
so you may want to cut them longer
to allow for piecing variations.

- ☐ White fabric, 1¼ yards (1.2 m)
- ☐ Red fabric, 1¼ yards (1.2 m)
- ☐ Thread for piecing
- ☐ Twin-size quilt batting
- ☐ Binding fabric, ⅝ yard (0.6 m)
- ☐ Backing fabric, 2¾ yards (2.5 m)

Duck, Duck, Goose was a favorite schoolyard game of mine growing up, so I decided to borrow the name for this quilt. Although the game goes by different names depending on where you live, according to one legend the original version of Duck, Duck, Goose was invented in the 1700s. Sadly, the game's inventor was playing in the mountains one day and fell off a cliff while chasing the "goose." Fortunately, you will have a much happier ending when you complete this project.

CUTTING INSTRUCTIONS

Measurements include ¼" (6 mm) seam allowances.

From white fabric, cut:

- ☐ (2) 6⅞" (17.5 cm) × WOF (width-of-fabric) strips; subcut into (6) 6⅞" (17.5 cm) squares; subcut diagonally to create 12 half-square triangles

- ☐ (1) 6½" (16.5 cm) × WOF strip; subcut into (5) 6½" (16.5 cm) squares

- ☐ (8) 2½" (6.5 cm) × WOF strips; subcut the strips into 2½" × 30½" (6.5 cm × 77.5 cm) strips for outside borders and strip sets

From red fabric, cut:

- ☐ (2) 6⅞" (17.5 cm) × WOF strips; subcut into (6) 6⅞" (17.5 cm) squares; subcut diagonally to create 12 half-square triangles

- ☐ (6) 2½" (6.5 cm) × WOF strips; subcut 4 of the strips into 2½" × 30½" (6.5 cm × 77.5 cm) strips for outside borders and strip sets

- ☐ (1) 6½" (16.5 cm) × WOF strip; subcut into (5) 6½" (16.5 cm) squares

- ☐ (5) 2½" (6.5cm) × WOF strips for binding

BLOCK ASSEMBLY

1. Following the directions in chapter 2, sew 1 Goose in the Pond block (FIGURE 1).

2. From the leftover portion of strip set 1 from the Goose in the Pond block, cut an additional (8) 2½" (6.5 cm) units.

3. From the leftover portion of strip set 2 of the Goose in the Pond block, cut an additional (4) 2½" (6.5 cm) units.

FIGURE 1

FIGURE 2

FIGURE 3

FIGURE 4

4. Sew 1 white/red/white rectangle between 2 red/white/red rectangles to make a Nine Patch unit (FIGURE 2). Press seams open. Make 4 Nine Patch units.

WALL HANGING ASSEMBLY

5. Sew together (3) 2½" × 30½" (6.5 cm × 77.5 cm) strips in this order: 1 white, 1 red, and 1 white (FIGURE 3). Press seams open. Make 4 border strip sets.

6. Sew 1 Nine Patch unit to each end of 2 of the strip sets from step 5 to create the top and bottom borders (FIGURE 4). Press seams open.

7. Referring to FIGURE 5, sew 1 border strip set to each side of the Goose in the Pond block. Press seams open. Sew the top and bottom borders to the block. Press seams open.

FINISHING THE WALL HANGING

8. Divide the backing into (2) 50" (127 cm) × WOF panels. Remove the selvedges. Cut 1 panel in half. Join 1 narrower panel to either side of the 50" (127 cm) wide panel.

9. Layer the backing (right-side down), batting, and quilt top (right-side up); baste. Quilt as desired.

10. Join the 2¼" (5.5 cm) binding strips into one continuous piece for straight-grain French-fold binding (see French-Fold Binding in chapter 1). Add the binding to the quilt.

FIGURE 5

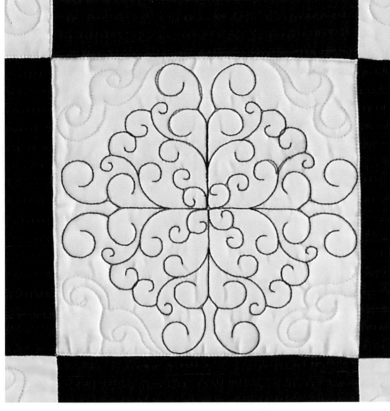

VARIATIONS

You can use any (2) 30" (76 cm) blocks to create this design, such as Carpenter's Square blocks (VARIATION 1) or Princess Feather blocks (VARIATION 2).

VARIATION 1

VARIATION 2

FOUR-LEAF CLOVER
PILLOW SHAM

PIECED AND MACHINE-QUILTED BY Linda Pumphrey.

FINISHED SIZE: 24" (61 cm) square

MATERIALS

Yardages are based on 40–42" (101.5–106.5 cm) wide fabric. Border strips are the exact length needed, so you may want to cut them longer to allow for piecing variations.

- ☐ Red fabric, 1⅛ yards (1 m)
- ☐ White fabric, 1½ yards (1.4 m)
- ☐ Craft-size quilt batting
- ☐ Pillow form, 24" (61 cm) square
- ☐ Paper-backed fusible web, ⅜ yard (0.4 m)
- ☐ Thread for piecing
- ☐ Four-Leaf Clover block templates (on CD)

Coordinate your pillow sham to match your quilt or use one that is different but complements your bedding. This pillow sham is simple to make and offers an easy way to update a room. Plus, start your day off with the good luck of a four-leaf clover.

Did you know that each leaf of the four-leaf clover has a meaning? The first is for faith, the second for hope, the third for love, and the fourth for luck. The mystique of the four-leaf clover dates back to the earliest stories of mankind when it is thought that Eve carried a four-leaf clover out of the Garden of Eden.

CUTTING INSTRUCTIONS

Measurements include ¼"
(6 mm) seam allowances. Follow
manufacturer's directions for
fusing the paper-backed fusible web to the "pre-fused" red
fabric before cutting fabric.

From white fabric, cut:

☐ (1) 14" (35.5 cm) × WOF
(width-of-fabric) strip; subcut
into (1)14" (35.5 cm) square

☐ (1) 27" (68.5 cm) square
for pillow backing

☐ From remaining fabric, cut (1) 8"
(20.5 cm) × WOF strip; subcut
into (4) 8" (20.5 cm) squares

From red fabric, cut:

☐ (2) 6½" (16.5 cm) × WOF
strips; subcut (4) 6½" × 12½"
(16.5 cm × 31.5 cm) rectangles

☐ (1) 24½" (62 cm) × WOF strip;
subcut into (2) 20" × 24½"
(51 cm × 62 cm) rectangles

From "pre-fused" red fabric, cut:

☐ 32 part A for the Four-Leaf Clover
blocks and corner blocks

BLOCK ASSEMBLY

1. Following the instructions in
chapter 2, make 1 Four-Leaf Clover
block (FIGURE 1). Square up and
trim to 12½" (31.5) square.

CORNER BLOCK ASSEMBLY

1. Locate the center of each 8"
(20.5 cm) white square by folding the fabric square diagonally
in fourths and diagonally in both
directions and creasing lightly.

FIGURE 1

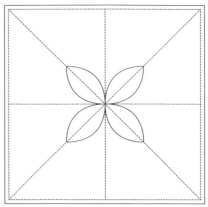

FIGURE 2

FIGURE 3

NOTE: *Be careful not to stretch the
square when folding on the bias.*

2. Press 4 part A shapes in the
center of each square following the
diagonal lines as shown (FIGURE 2)
to make a Corner unit. Appliqué
the shapes. Square up and trim the
units to 6½" (16.5 cm) square.

ASSEMBLING THE PILLOW TOP

Refer to FIGURE 3 throughout assembly.

3. Sew (1) 6½" × 12½" (16.5 cm
× 31.5 cm) red rectangle to opposite sides of the Four-Leaf Clover
block. Press the seams open.

4. Sew 1 Corner unit to each short side of the 6½" × 12½" (16.5 cm × 31.5 cm) remaining red rectangles to complete top and bottom borders. Press the seams open. Sew the top and bottom borders to the block. Press the seams open.

5. Layer the pillow top, batting, and backing together. Pin baste the layers together to secure them in place. Machine quilt as desired.

FINISHING THE PILLOW SHAM

6. Trim excess batting and backing around the pillow top. It should measure about 24½" (62 cm) square (some shrinkage might have occurred from the quilting).

7. Hem both 20" × 24½" (51 cm × 62 cm) rectangles along one long edge. First, fold under ½" (1.3 cm) to the wrong side and press. Fold under ½" (1.3 cm) again and press, then sew with a straight stitch.

8. With right sides together and the design of the pillow upright, pin 1 pillow back piece to the top half of the quilted pillow top. Add the other pillow back piece to the bottom half of the quilted pillow top so the hemmed edges of the pillow back overlap. Sew around the pillow edges through all layers using a ¼" (6 mm) seam allowance. Clip the corners.

9. Turn the pillow right-side out. Smooth the pillow cover and insert a 24" (61 cm) pillow form.

VARIATIONS

You can use any 12" (30.5 cm) block for the center square, such as the Nine Patch block with leaves in the corners (VARIATION 1) or the Mirror Image block with leaves in the corners (VARIATION 2).

VARIATION 1

VARIATION 2

HEART HANDKERCHIEF
WALL HANGING

PIECED AND APPLIQUÉD BY **Linda Pumphrey**. MACHINE-QUILTED BY **Karen Kielmeyer**.

FINISHED SIZE: 56" (142 cm) square

MATERIALS

Yardages are based on 40–42" (101.5–106.5 cm) wide fabric. Border strips are the exact length needed, so you may want to cut them longer to allow for piecing variations.

☐ White fabric, 2⅛ yards (2 m)

☐ Red fabric, 3 yards (2.8 m)

☐ Featherweight interfacing, 3¾ yards (3.4 m)

☐ Paper-backed fusible web, 4½ yards (4.1 m)

☐ Thread for piecing

☐ Thread for appliqué

☐ Backing fabric, 3⅝ yard (3.3 m)

☐ Binding fabric, ⅝ yard (0.6 m)

☐ Twin-size quilt batting

☐ Handkerchief block templates (on CD)

Cloth handkerchiefs are thought to have been first used by King Richard II of England when he used plain pieces of cloth. Since that time handkerchiefs have become very decorative with all sorts of designs. The heart shapes on the Handkerchief block gives a very romantic feel to the wall hanging. Repeating shapes on the corner of the border adds interest to what are otherwise plain borders.

AUTHOR TIP
Prevent Shadowing

When appliquéing lighter fabric on to darker fabric, line the lighter fabric with fusible feather-weight interfacing before adding paper-backed fusible web to prevent shadowing.

CUTTING INSTRUCTIONS

Measurements include ¼" (6 mm) seam allowances.

From white fabric, cut:

- ☐ (1) 59½" (151 cm) × WOF (width-of-fabric) strip; subcut (2) 1½" × 48" (3.8 cm × 122 cm) strips along the length and (2) 1½" × 50½" (3.8 cm × 128.5 cm) strips along the length for inside borders

- ☐ Line the back of the leftover white fabric with featherweight interfacing to prevent shadowing. Then fuse it to paper-backed fusible web.

From "pre-fused" white fabric, cut:

- ☐ 9 part E for Handkerchief block background shapes

- ☐ (4) 1½" (3.8 cm) squares for outer border corner motifs

From red fabric, cut:

- ☐ (1) 56½" (143.5 cm) × WOF (width-of-fabric) strips; subcut (2) 3½" × 50½" (9 cm × 128.5 cm) strips, (2) 3½" × 56½" (9 cm × 143.5 cm) strips, and (3) 18" (45.5 cm) squares

- ☐ (3) 18" (45.5 cm) × WOF; subcut into (6) 18" (45.5 cm) squares

- ☐ (7) 2¼" (5.7cm) × WOF strips for binding

From "pre-fused" red fabric, cut:

- ☐ 9 part A for the Handkerchief blocks

- ☐ 36 part B for the Handkerchief blocks

- ☐ 36 part C for the Handkerchief blocks

- ☐ 36 part D for the Handkerchief blocks

BLOCK ASSEMBLY

1. Following the instructions in chapter 2, make 9 Handkerchief blocks (FIGURE 1). Square up the blocks to 16½" (42 cm).

WALL HANGING ASSEMBLY

2. Sew 3 blocks together to make a row (FIGURE 2). Press the seams open. Make 3 rows.

3. Sew the rows together, matching the corners. Press seams open.

TIME-SAVER TIP

The following fabric cutting die can make the cutting process faster and more accurate:

- ■ For 2¼" (5.5 cm) bindings, use GO! Strip Cutter #55053 2¼" (5.5 cm) [Finished 1¾" (4.5 cm)]

FIGURE 1

FIGURE 2

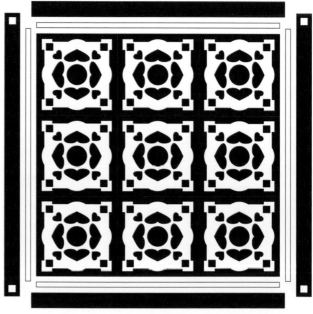

FIGURE 3

BORDER ASSEMBLY

Refer to FIGURE 3 for steps 4 and 5.

4. Sew (1) 1½" × 48" (3.8 cm × 122 cm) white strip to the top and bottom of the quilt. Press seams open. Then sew (1) 1½" × 50½" (3.8 cm × 128.5 cm) white border to each side. Press seams open.

5. Sew (1) 3½" × 50½" (9 cm × 128.5 cm) red border to the top and bottom of the quilt. Press seams open. Then sew (1) 3½" × 56½" (9 cm × 143.5 cm) red border to each side. Press seams open.

6. Press (1) 1½" (3.8 cm) pre-fused white square in each corner of the red border 1" (2.5 cm) from the edges. Appliqué in place using your favorite stitch and white thread.

FINISHING THE WALL HANGING

7. Divide the backing fabric into (2) 64" (162.5 cm) lengths. Remove the selvedges. Cut 1 piece in half lengthwise to make 2 narrower panels. Join 1 narrower panel to each long side of the wider panel. Press seams open.

8. Layer the backing (right-side down), batting, and quilt top (right-side up); baste. Quilt as desired.

9. Join the 2¼" (5.5 cm) binding strips into one continuous piece for straight-grain French-fold binding (see French-Fold Binding in chapter 1). Add binding to the quilt.

VARIATIONS

You can use any 16" (40.5 cm) blocks to create your own design, such as the Oak Reel Version Two blocks (VARIATION 1) or Seven Sisters blocks (VARIATION 2).

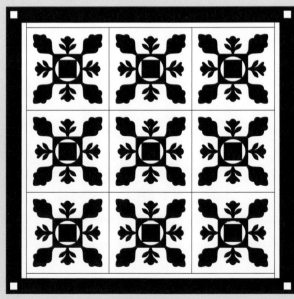

VARIATION 1

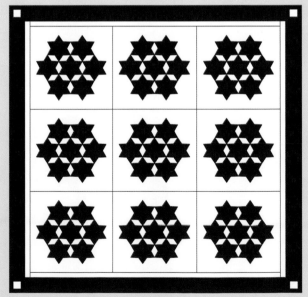

VARIATION 2

OUR VILLAGE GREEN
WALL HANGING

PIECED AND APPLIQUÉD BY **Linda Pumphrey.** MACHINE-QUILTED BY **Karen Kielmeyer.**

FINISHED SIZE: 94" (239 cm) square

MATERIALS

Yardages are based on 40–42" (101.5–106.5 cm) wide fabric. Border strips are the exact length needed, so you may want to cut them longer to allow for piecing variations.

- ☐ White fabric, 3⅜ yards (3.1 m)
- ☐ Red fabric, 4½ yards (4.1 m)
- ☐ Backing fabric, 4 yards (3.7 m)
- ☐ Binding fabric, ½ yard (0.5 m)
- ☐ Twin-size quilt batting
- ☐ Thread for piecing

This wall hanging reminds me of the song lyrics found in "Sporting on the Village Green" by Jane Taylor. The song starts with the following lines, "On the cheerful village green, Scattered round with houses neat. All the boys and girls are seen, Playing there with busy feet." The four center Our Village Green blocks are sewn on point surrounded by Unnamed blocks. The center white rectangles in the Unnamed block remind me of doors in the houses.

CUTTING INSTRUCTIONS

Measurements include ¼" (6 mm) seam allowances.

From white fabric, cut:

☐ (4) 1¼" (3.2 cm) × WOF strips (width-of-fabric) strips; subcut into (2) 1¼" × 36½" (3.2 cm × 93 cm) rectangles and (2) 1¼" × 34½" (3.8 cm × 87.5 cm) rectangles for inner white borders

☐ (4) 4¼" (11 cm) × WOF strips; subcut into (24) 4¼" (11 cm) squares; cut each square diagonally twice into 96 quarter-square triangles for Our Village Green blocks

☐ (10) 3¾" (9.5 cm) × WOF strips; subcut (96) 3¾" (9.5 cm) squares; cut each square diagonally to form 192 half-square triangles for Unnamed blocks

☐ (10) 5¼" (13.5 cm) × WOF strip; subcut into (32) 5¼" (13.5 cm) squares; cut each square in half diagonally twice to form 128 quarter-squares for Unnamed blocks

☐ (2) 2⅞" (7.5 cm) × WOF strips; subcut (32) 2⅞" (7.5 cm) squares; cut each square diagonally once to form 64 half-squares for corners for Unnamed blocks

From red fabric, cut:

☐ (1) 6½" (16.5 cm) × WOF strips; subcut into (4) 6½" (16.5 cm) squares for Our Village Green block centers

☐ (4) 4¼" (11 cm) × WOF strips; subcut into (24) 4¼" (11 cm) squares; cut each square diagonally twice into 96 quarter-square triangles for Our Village Green blocks

☐ (10) 3¾" (9.5 cm) × WOF strips; subcut (96) 3¾" (9.5 cm) squares; cut each square diagonally to make 192 half-square triangles for Unnamed blocks

☐ (10) 5¼" (13.5 cm) × WOF strips; subcut into (32) 5¼" (13.5 cm) squares; cut each square in half diagonally twice to form 128 quarter-squares for Unnamed blocks

☐ (1) 18¼ strip (46.5 cm); subcut into (2) 18¼ strip (46.5 cm) squares; cut each square diagonally to create 4 half-square triangles for setting triangles

☐ (6) 2¼" (5.5 cm) × WOF strips for binding

TIME-SAVER TIP

The following fabric cutting dies can make the cutting process faster and more accurate:

- For 2¼" (5.5 cm) bindings, use GO! Strip Cutter #55053 2¼" (5.5 cm) [Finished 1¾" (4.5 cm)]

- For 1½" (3.8 cm) for logs, use GO! Strip Cutter #55024 1½" (3.8 cm) [Finished 1" (2.5 cm)]

- For 1¼" (3.2 cm) strips, use GO! Strip Cutter #55109 1¼" (3.2 cm) [Finished ¾" (2 cm)]

- For 3" (7.5 cm) squares, use GO! Square Cutter #55256 3" (3.2 cm) [Finished 2½" (6.5 cm)]

- For 6½" (16.5 cm) squares, use GO! Square #55000 6½" (16.5 cm) [6" (15 cm)]

FIGURE 1

FIGURE 2

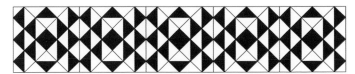

FIGURE 3

FIGURE 4   FIGURE 5

FIGURE 6

FIGURE 7

BLOCK ASSEMBLY

1. Following the instructions in chapter 2, make 4 Our Village Green blocks (FIGURE 1) and 16 Unnamed blocks (FIGURE 2).

WALL HANGING ASSEMBLY

2. Sew together 5 Unnamed blocks as shown (FIGURE 3), noting the orientation of the blocks. Press seams open. Make 2 rows.

3. Sew together 3 Unnamed blocks for Side units (FIGURE 4), noting the orientation of the blocks. Press seams open. Make 2 rows.

4. Sew together 2 Our Village Green Blocks. Press seams open. Make 2 rows. Sew the rows together as shown to make the center medallion. Press seams open (FIGURE 5).

5. Referring to FIGURE 6, sew 1 half-square triangle to each side of the center medallion. Press the seams towards the half-square triangles. Sew (1) 1½" × 34½" (3.2 cm × 87.5 cm) strip to the top and bottom of the center medallion and (1) 1¼" × 36½" (3.2cm x 93cm) strip to each side of the center medallion. Press the seams open.

6. Sew the Side units to the center medallion as shown (FIGURE 7). Press seams open.

7. Referring to FIGURE 8, sew the top and bottom Unnamed block rows units to the middle section. Press seams open.

FINISHING THE WALL HANGING

8. Divide the backing into (2) 68" (172.5 cm) × WOF lengths. Remove the selvedges. Divide 1 length in half lengthwise and join to either side of the wider panel. Press seams open.

9. Layer the backing (right-side down), batting, and quilt top (right-side up); baste. Quilt as desired.

10. Join the 2¼" (5.5 cm) binding strips into one continuous piece for straight-grain French-fold binding (see French-Fold Binding in chapter 1). Add the binding to the quilt.

FIGURE 8

VARIATIONS

You can use any of the 12" (30.5 cm) blocks in this setting, such as Five Quarter-Square (VARIATION 1) and Garden Maze blocks or Courthouse Steps and Stars blocks (VARIATION 2).

VARIATION 1

VARIATION 2

Ocean Wave
1840–1983
Makers: Mrs. Kennedy and Ardis James
48" × 62" (128 cm × 157.5 cm)

RING AROUND THE ROSY
WALL HANGING

PIECED AND APPLIQUÉD BY **Linda Pumphrey.** MACHINE-QUILTED BY **Karen Kielmeyer.**

FINISHED SIZE: 52" (132 cm) square

MATERIALS

Yardages are based on 40–42" (101.5–106.5 cm) wide fabric. Border strips are the exact length needed, so you may want to cut them longer to allow for piecing variations.

☐ White fabric, 2½ yards (2.3 m)

☐ Red fabric, 1½ yards (1.4 m)

☐ Backing fabric, 3⅓ yards (3 m)

☐ Binding fabric, ½ yard (0.5 m)

☐ Twin-size quilt batting

☐ Paper-backed fusible web, 3½ yards (3.2 m)

☐ Fusible featherweight interfacing, ¼ yard (0.2 m) (optional)

☐ Thread for piecing

☐ Thread for appliqué

☐ Oak Reel block and Wagon Wheel block templates (on CD)

The nursery rhyme and game Ring around the Rosy is thought to be a child's version of a ring dance. Reel dances or "ring dances" trace their history back to the Druids, who danced in religious rituals honoring the oak tree. It seems fitting in this quilt that the Oak Reel blocks are dancing around a circular Wagon Wheel block. When looking at this quilt, you can almost hear the children singing.

CUTTING INSTRUCTIONS

Measurements include ¼"
(6 mm) seam allowances.

From white fabric, cut:

☐ (4) 14" (35.5 cm) × WOF (width-of-fabric) strips; subcut (12) 14" (35.5 cm) squares

☐ (2) 2½" (6.5 cm) ×WOF strips; subcut each strip into (1) 2½" × 16½" (6.5 cm × 42 cm) and (1) 2½" × 20½" (6.5 cm × 52 cm) rectangles for white inner border

☐ (1) 18" (45.5 cm)× WOF strip; subcut into (1) 18" (45.5 cm) square

☐ (1) 5" (12.5 cm) × LOF (length-of-fabric) strip; apply paper-backed fusible web for cutting out appliqué shapes, then line with lightweight interfacing to prevent shadowing (optional)

From "pre-fused" white fabric, cut:

☐ 8 part C for the spoke of Wagon Wheel block

☐ 1 part B (3" [7.5 cm] circle) of the Wagon Wheel block

From red fabric, cut:

☐ (1) 52½" (133.5 cm) × LOF strip; subcut (2) 2½" × 52½" (6.5 cm × 133.5 cm) strips, (2) 2½" × 48½" (6.5 cm × 123 cm) strips for outside borders. For inside borders, cut (2) 2½" × 24½" (6.5 cm × 62 cm) strips and (2) 2½" × 20½" (6.5 cm × 52 cm) strips

☐ Apply paper-backed fusible web to remaining red fabric to create "pre-fused" fabric for cutting out appliqué shapes.

From "pre-fused" red fabric, cut:

☐ 48 part A for the Oak Reel blocks

☐ 1 part A (13" [33 cm] circle) for the Wagon Wheel block

☐ 48 part B for the Oak Reel blocks

☐ 12 part C for the Oak Reel blocks

BLOCK ASSEMBLY

1. Following the instructions in chapter 2, make 12 Oak Reel blocks (FIGURE 1) and 1 Wagon Wheel block (FIGURE 2). Square up and trim the Oak Reel blocks to 12½" (31.5 cm) square and the Wagon Wheel block to 16½" (42 cm) square.

FIGURE 1

FIGURE 2

FIGURE 3

FIGURE 4

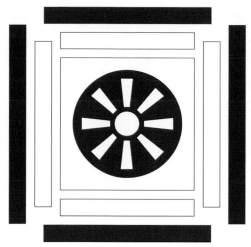

FIGURE 5

FIGURE 6

WALL HANGING ASSEMBLY

2. Sew 4 Oak Reel blocks together. Press seams open (FIGURE 3). Make 2 rows.

3. Sew 2 Oak Reel blocks together for the Side units. Press seam open (FIGURE 4). Make 2 Side units.

4. Referring to FIGURE 5, add the inner borders. Sew (1) 2½" × 16½" (6.5 cm × 42 cm) white strip to the top and 1 to the bottom of the Wagon Wheel block. Press seams open. Sew (1) 2½" × 20½" (6.5 cm × 52 cm) white strip to each side. Press seams open. Sew (1) 2½" × 20½" (6.5 cm × 52 cm) red strip to the top and bottom. Press seams open. Then sew (1) 2½" × 24½" (6.5 cm × 62 cm) red strip to each side. Press seams open.

5. Sew 1 Oak Reel Side unit to either side of the quilt center (FIGURE 6). Press the seams toward the red inner border.

8. Sew (1) 4-block Oak Reel Row unit to the top of the quilt center and 1 to the bottom. Press the seams toward the red inner border.

9. Referring to FIGURE 7, sew (1) 2½" × 48½" (6.5 cm × 123 cm) red strip to the top and 1 to the bottom of the quilt. Press seams toward the red border. Then sew (1) 2½" × 52½" (6.5 cm × 133.5 cm) red strip to each side (FIGURE 8). Press seams toward the red border.

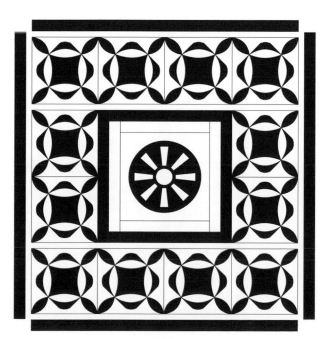

FIGURE 7

FINISHING THE WALL HANGING

10. Divide the backing into (2) 60" (152.5 cm) × WOF lengths. Remove the selvedges. Divide 1 length in half lengthwise and join to either side of the wider panel. Press seams open.

11. Layer the backing (right-side down), batting, and quilt top (right-side up); baste. Quilt as desired.

13. Join the 2¼" (5.5 cm) binding strips into one continuous piece for straight-grain French-fold binding (see French-Fold Binding in chapter 1). Add the binding to the quilt.

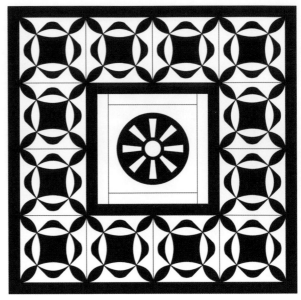

FIGURE 8

VARIATIONS

You can use any combination of 12" (30.5 cm) and 16" (40.5 cm) blocks in this delightful setting, such as the 12" (30.5 cm) Diamonds block and 16" (40.5 cm) Seven Sisters block (VARIATION 1) or the 12" (30.5 cm) Snowflake block and 16" (40.5 cm) Handkerchief block (VARIATION 2).

VARIATION 1

VARIATION 2

PICK THREE
TABLE RUNNER

PIECED AND MACHINE-QUILTED BY Linda Pumphrey.

FINISHED SIZE: 17½" × 51½"
(44.5 cm × 131 cm)

MATERIALS

Yardages are based on 40–42"
(101.5–106.5 cm) wide fabric.

- ☐ White fabric, 1½ yards (1.4 m)
- ☐ Red fabric, 1⅜ yards (1.2 m)
- ☐ Backing fabric, 1¾ yards (1.6 m)
- ☐ Crib-size quilt batting
- ☐ Thread for piecing

Sampler quilts have been popular since the mid-1800s. They are a great way to use blocks left over from other projects, audition a new block, or try a new technique. With this design, you can pick any three of your favorite 12" (30.5 cm) blocks and display them as a centerpiece on your table. This runner is also fabulous when showcasing three of the same block design in a repeating pattern.

CUTTING INSTRUCTIONS

Measurements include ¼" (6 mm) seam allowances. Follow manufacturer's directions for fusing the paper-backed fusible web to the "pre-fused" red fabric before cutting fabric.

From white fabric, cut:

☐ (1) 18¼" (46.5 cm) × WOF (width-of-fabric) strips; subcut into (1) 18¼" (46.5 cm) square; cut the square in half diagonally twice to make 4 setting triangles

☐ (1) 5¼" (13.5 cm) × WOF strip; subcut (2) 5¼" (13.5 cm) squares, then cut each square diagonally twice to create 8 quarter-square triangles; from the remaining portion of strip, subcut (4) 4½" (11.5 cm) squares for Ohio Star block

☐ (1) 3¼" (8.5 cm) × WOF strip; subcut into (2) 3¼" (8.5 cm) squares, then cut each square in half diagonally to make 4 half-squares for the block Corner units for Wild Goose Chase; from the remaining portion of the strip, subcut (12) 2⅝" (6.5 cm) squares; cut each square in half diagonally to make 24 half-squares for Flying Geese units for the Wild Goose Chase block

☐ (1) 8⅜" (21.5 cm) square; subcut the square in half diagonally twice to make 4 quarter-square triangles for the block sides for the Wild Goose Chase block

☐ (2) 2⅝" (6.5 cm) × WOF strips; subcut (2) 2⅝" (6.5 cm) squares and (1) 2⅝" × 7" (6.5 cm × 18 cm) rectangle for Chimney Sweep block

☐ (1) 3⅜" (8.5 cm) × WOF strip; subcut (3) 3⅜" (8.5 cm) squares, then cut each square in half diagonally twice to make 12 quarter-square triangles; from the remaining portion of the strip, subcut (2) 3" (7.5 cm) squares; cut squares in half diagonally to make 4 half-square triangles for the Chimney Sweep block

From red fabric, cut:

☐ (1) 5¼" (13.5 cm) × WOF strip; subcut (2) 5¼" (13.5 cm) squares, then cut the squares diagonally twice to create 8 quarter-square triangles; from the remaining portion of the strip, subcut (1) 4½" (11.5 cm) square for the Ohio Star block

☐ (2) 3⅞" (10 cm) × WOF strips; subcut (1) 3⅞" (10 cm) square; from the remaining strip subcut (6) 3¼" (8.5 cm) squares, cut squares in half diagonally to make 12 half-squares for Flying Geese units for the Wild Goose Chase block

☐ (1) 2⅝" (6.5 cm) × WOF strips; subcut (8) 2⅝" (6.5 cm) squares and (4) 2⅝" × 7" (6.5 cm × 18 cm) rectangles for the Chimney Sweep block

☐ (4) 2¼" (5.5 cm) × WOF strips for binding

From "pre-fused" red fabric, cut:

☐ (3) 1¼" (3.2 cm) × WOF strips; subcut into (4) 12½" (31.5 cm) strips

---

VARIATIONS

You can use any combination of 12" (30.5 cm) blocks in this delightful setting, such as a combination of the Basket, Eight of Hearts, and Small Basket blocks (VARIATION 1) or 3 Lobster blocks (VARIATION 2).

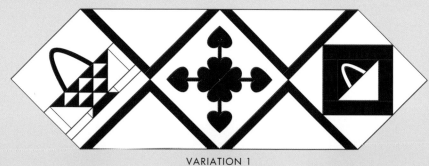

VARIATION 1

VARIATION 2

FIGURE 1

FIGURE 2

BLOCK ASSEMBLY

1. Following the instructions in chapter 2, sew 1 each of the Ohio Star (FIGURE 1), Wild Goose Chase (FIGURE 2), and Chimney Sweep (FIGURE 3) blocks.

2. Press and appliqué the 1¼" (3.2 cm) wide "pre-fused red" strips on each short side of the 4 setting triangles (FIGURE 4). Trim the ends (FIGURE 5).

FIGURE 3

TABLE RUNNER TOP ASSEMBLY

3. Lay out the 3 diagonal rows as shown (FIGURE 6). Sew the rows together. Press seams away from the appliquéd edges.

FIGURE 4

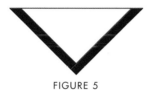

FIGURE 5

FINISHING THE RUNNER

4. Trim the backing to 22½" × 59½" (57 cm × 151 cm).

5. Layer the backing (right-side down), batting, and quilt top (right-side up); baste. Quilt as desired.

6. Join the 2¼" (5.5 cm) binding strips into one continuous piece for straight-grain French-fold binding (see French-Fold Binding in chapter 1). Add the binding to the quilt.

FIGURE 6

FIGURE 7

SIMPLY TOUCHING STARS QUILT

PIECED AND APPLIQUÉD BY **Linda Pumphrey**. MACHINE-QUILTED BY **Karen Kielmeyer**.

FINISHED SIZE: **96"** (244 cm) square

MATERIALS

Yardages are based on 40–42" (101.6–106.7 cm) wide fabric.

☐ White fabric, 4¼ yards (3.9 m)
☐ Red fabric, 9 yards (8.3 m)
☐ Backing fabric, 9 yards (8.2 m)
☐ Binding fabric, 1 yard (0.9 m)
☐ King-size quilt batting
☐ Thread for piecing

"Dreams are like stars. You may never touch them, but if you follow them they will lead you to your destiny." —ANONYMOUS

The simple arrangement of four blocks placed together is made a little more intricate by adding pieced or appliquéd setting blocks. Four-block quilts were popular in quiltmaking between 1850 and 1900. The same motif repeated created the overall design. For this contemporary version, a pieced block called Simple Design was added in the corner squares.

CUTTING INSTRUCTIONS

Measurements include ¼"
(6 mm) seam allowances.

From white fabric, cut:

- ☐ (40) 2½" (6.5 cm) × WOF (width-of-fabric) strips for Touching Stars blocks

- ☐ (4) 4⅞" (12.5 cm) × WOF strips; subcut into (30) 4⅞" (12.5 cm) squares; subcut each square diagonally to create 60 half-square triangles for Simple Design blocks

- ☐ (2) 8⅞" (22.5 cm) × WOF strips; subcut into (6) 8⅞" (22.5 cm) squares; subcut each square diagonally to create 12 half-square triangles for Simple Design blocks

From red fabric, cut:

- ☐ (52) 2½" (6.5 cm) × WOF strips for Touching Stars blocks

- ☐ (20) 1½" × WOF strips; subcut 8 strips into (24) 1½" × 12½" (3.8 cm × 31.5 cm) rectangles; subcut 12 strips into (24) 1½" × 14½" (3.8 cm × 37 cm) rectangles for Simple Design block frames

- ☐ (4) 4⅞" (12.5 cm) × WOF strips; subcut into (30) 4⅞" (12.5 cm) squares; subcut each square diagonally to create 60 half-square triangles for Simple Design blocks

- ☐ (2) 8⅞" (22.5 cm) × WOF strips; subcut into (6) 8⅞" (22.5 cm) squares; subcut diagonally to create 12 half-square triangles for Simple Design blocks

- ☐ (4) 21¼" (54 cm) × WOF strips; subcut (4) 21¼" (54 cm) squares; subcut each square diagonally twice to create 16 quarter-square triangles for Touching Stars blocks side setting triangles

- ☐ (2) 14½" (37 cm) × WOF strips; subcut into (4) 14½" (37 cm) squares for red corner blocks

FIGURE 1

FIGURE 2

FIGURE 3

FIGURE 4

BLOCK ASSEMBLY

1. Following the instructions in chapter 2, make 4 Touching Stars blocks with the following exception: do not sew in the Corner Square units (FIGURE 1). This will be done in step 4 of the Quilt Assembly.

2. Following the instructions in Chapter 2, piece 12 Simple Design blocks (FIGURE 2).

QUILT ASSEMBLY

3. Sew (1) 1½" × 12½" (3.8 cm × 31.5 cm) strip to the top and bottom of each Simple Design block. Then sew (1) 1½" × 14½" (3.8 cm × 37 cm) strip to each side (FIGURE 3). Press seams toward the red border.

4. Referring to FIGURE 4, sew 1 Simple Design block unit in 3 corners of each Touching Stars block. In the fourth corner, sew (1) 14½" (37 cm) red square. (See Sewing Y-Seams in chapter 1 for tips.)

5. Sew 2 blocks together for each row. Then sew the rows together.

FINISHING THE QUILT

6. Divide the backing into (3) 90" (228.5 cm) × WOF lengths. Remove the selvedges and sew panels together. Press seams open.

7. Layer the backing (right-side down), batting, and quilt top (right-side up); baste. Quilt as desired.

8. Join the 2¼" (5.5 cm) binding strips into one continuous piece for straight-grain French-fold binding (see French-Fold Binding in chapter 1). Add the binding to the quilt.

VARIATIONS

You can pair the 48" (122 cm) Touching Stars block with any 12" (30.5 cm) blocks in this delightful setting, such as the Courthouse Steps (VARIATION 1) or Snowflake (VARIATION 2).

VARIATION 1

VARIATION 2

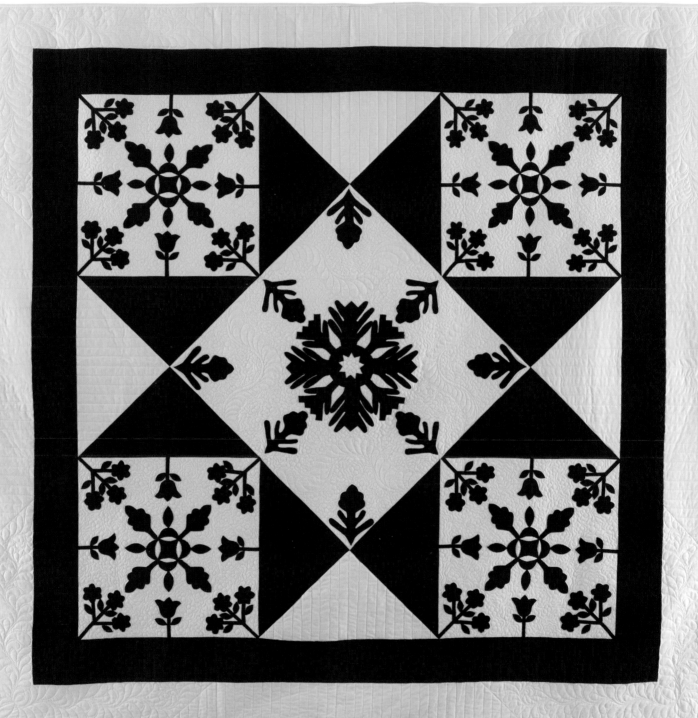

STARRY FLOWER GARDEN QUILT

PIECED AND APPLIQUÉD BY **Linda Pumphrey**. MACHINE-QUILTED BY **Karen Kielmeyer**.

FINISHED SIZE: 80" (203 cm) square

MATERIALS

Yardages are based on 40–42" (101.5–106.5 cm) wide fabric. Border strips are the exact length needed, so you may want to cut them longer to allow for piecing variations.

☐ White fabric, 4⅔ yards (4.3 m)

☐ Red fabric, 4 yards (3.7 m)

☐ Backing fabric, 7⅓ yards (6.7 m)

☐ Binding fabric, ¾ yard (0.7 m)

☐ Queen-size quilt batting

☐ Paper-backed fusible web, 4 yards (3.7 m)

☐ Thread for piecing

☐ Thread for appliqué

☐ Oak Reel and Flowers block and Paper Cut Appliqué block templates (on CD)

This quilt reminds me of Victor Hugo's quote from *Les Misérables*, "A garden to walk in and immensity to dream in—what more could he ask? A few flowers at his feet and above him the stars."

Starry Eye flowers are a simple five-petal flower seen in the Oak Reel and Flower block. Paired with the complex Paper Cut Appliqué block and surrounded by an oversized Ohio Star block, this quilt has a bold, contemporary look.

CUTTING INSTRUCTIONS

Measurements include ¼" (6 mm) seam allowances. Follow manufacturer's directions for fusing the paper-backed fusible web to the "pre-fused" red fabric before cutting fabric.

From white fabric, cut:

☐ (1) 90" (228.5 cm) length and (1) 72" (183) length

☐ From the 90" (228.5 cm) length, cut (2) 5½" (14 cm) × LOF (length-of-fabric) strips; subcut (2) 5½" × 80½" (14 cm × 204.5 cm) strips for side borders; from the remaining WOF (width-of-fabric) strip, cut (4) 22" (56 cm) squares for Oak Reel and Flowers blocks

☐ From the 72" (183 cm) length, cut (2) 5½" (14 cm) × LOF strips; subcut (2) 5½" × 70½" (14 cm × 179 cm) strips for top and bottom borders; from the remaining width of fabric, cut (1) 22" (56 cm) square for Paper Cut Appliqué block and (2) 21¼" (54 cm) squares; subcut the 21¼" (54 cm) squares diagonally twice to form 8 quarter-square triangles each

From red fabric, cut:

☐ (1) 72" (183 cm) length and (1) 62" (157.5 cm) length

☐ From the 72" (183 cm) length, cut (2) 5½" (14 cm) × LOF strips; subcut (2) 5½" × 70½" (14 cm × 179 cm) strips for inner side borders; from the remaining width of fabric, cut (2) 21¼" (54 cm) squares; subcut the 21¼" (54 cm) squares diagonally twice to form 8 quarter-square triangles

☐ From the 62" (157.5 cm) length, cut (2) 5½" (14 cm) × LOF strips; subcut (2) 5½" × 60½" (14 cm × 153.5 cm) strips for inner top and bottom borders

NOTE: *Use the balance of the red fabric for the "pre-fused" fabric. Lightly label the back of each part and separate the parts by block.*

From "pre-fused" red fabric, cut:

☐ 96 part D for Oak Reel and Flowers blocks

☐ 48 part B for the Oak Reel and Flowers blocks

☐ 16 part A for Oak Reel and Flowers blocks

☐ 16 part E for Oak Reel and Flowers blocks

☐ 16 part C for Oak Reel and Flowers blocks

☐ 4 part F for Oak Reel and Flowers blocks

☐ 4 part G for Oak Reel and Flowers blocks

☐ 8 part D for Paper Cut Appliqué blocks

VARIATIONS

This quilt would also be delightful using only the Oak Reel and Flowers block (VARIATION 1) or using only the Paper Cut Appliqué block (VARIATION 2).

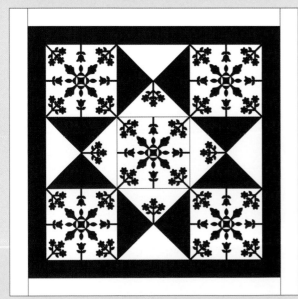

VARIATION 1

VARIATION 2

- ☐ 4 part B for Paper Cut Appliqué blocks
- ☐ 4 part C for Paper Cut Appliqué blocks
- ☐ 1 circle part A for Paper Cut Appliqué blocks

From white binding fabric, cut:

- ☐ (9) 2¼" (5.5 cm) strips

BLOCK ASSEMBLY

1. Following the directions in chapter 2, make 4 Oak Reel and Flowers blocks (FIGURE 1) and 1 Paper Cut Appliqué block (FIGURE 2).

QUILT TOP ASSEMBLY

2. Referring to FIGURE 3, sew together 1 red quarter-square triangle and 1 white quarter-square triangle. Make 8 units of each. Press the seams open. Sew 2 halves together to make Quarter-Square unit. Make 4 units.

3. Appliqué 1 red part D on an inside corner of each Quarter-Square unit with the stem pointing to the center of the block as shown (FIGURE 4).

4. Sew the blocks together in rows as follows (FIGURE 5):

▸ **ROWS 1 AND 3:** Sew together in this order, 1 Oak Reel and Flowers block, 1 Quarter-Square unit with the flower pointing down, and 1 Oak Reel and Flower block.

▸ **ROW 2:** Sew together in this order, 1 Quarter-Square unit with the flower pointing toward the center, 1 Paper Cut Appliqué block, and 1 Quarter-Square unit with the flower pointing toward the center.

Sew the 3 rows together making sure flowers are pointing toward the center of the quilt top.

FIGURE 1

FIGURE 2

FIGURE 3

FIGURE 4

FIGURE 5

BORDER ASSEMBLY

5. Referring to FIGURE 6, sew the 5½" × 60½" (14 cm × 153.7 cm) red inside borders to the top and bottom of the center panel. Then sew the 5½" × 70½" (14 cm × 179 cm) red inside borders to each side.

6. Sew (1) 5½" × 70½" (14 cm × 179 cm) white strip to the top and 1 to the bottom of the center panel for the outside borders. Sew (1) 5½" × 80½" (14 cm × 204.5 cm) white border to each side (FIGURE 7).

FINISHING THE QUILT

7. Divide backing into (3) 88" (223.5 cm) × WOF lengths. Remove the selvedges and sew panels together. Press seams open.

8. Layer the backing (right-side down), batting, and quilt top (right-side up); baste. Quilt as desired.

9. Join the 2¼" (5.5 cm) binding fabric into one continuous piece for straight-grain French-fold binding (see French-Fold Binding in chapter 1). Add the binding to the quilt.

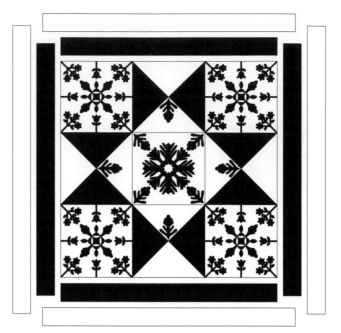

FIGURE 6

FIGURE 7

WINTER TIME QUILT

PIECED AND APPLIQUÉD BY **Linda Pumphrey**. MACHINE-QUILTED BY **Karen Kielmeyer.**

FINISHED SIZE: 84"
(213.5 cm) square

MATERIALS

Yardages are based on 40–42"
(101.6–106.7 cm) wide fabric. Border
strips are the exact length needed,
so you may want to cut them longer
to allow for piecing variations.

- ☐ White fabric, 7½ yards (6.9 m)
- ☐ Red fabric, 6¼ yards (5.7 m)
- ☐ Backing fabric, 7⅔ yards (7 m)
- ☐ Binding fabric, ¾ yard (0.7 m)
- ☐ Queen-size quilt batting
- ☐ Paper-backed fusible web,
  3½ yards (3.2 m)
- ☐ Thread for piecing
- ☐ Thread for appliqué
- ☐ Snowflake block and Cactus
  Flower block templates (on CD)

Do you love quilts where the blocks create a secondary design once they are put together? Then this "Snowflake Cactus" quilt pattern is for you. The two blocks Cactus Flower and Snowflake are inspired by an Album quilt in the International Quilt Study Center & Museum's collection that was made in Boston, Massachusetts, and dated from 1850. Both blocks are interesting and striking on their own. Paired together, they create an eye-catching secondary design.

CUTTING INSTRUCTIONS

Measurements include ¼" (6 mm) seam allowances. Follow manufacturer's directions for fusing the paper-backed fusible web to the "pre-fused" red fabric before cutting fabric.

From white fabric, cut:

☐ (1) 80½" (204.5 cm) × LOF (length-of-fabric) strips; subcut (2) 2½" × 80½" (6.5 cm × 204.5 cm) and (2) 2½" × 76½" (6.5 cm × 194.5 cm) strips for middle outside borders; from remaining fabric cut (2) 14" × LOF strips; subcut (10) 14" (35.5 cm) squares from each strip

☐ (13) 14" (35.5 cm) × WOF (width-of-fabric) strips; subcut (26) 14" (35.5 cm) squares

From red fabric, cut:

☐ (1) 84½" (214.5 cm) × LOF strip; subcut (2) 2½" × 84½" (6.5 cm × 214.5 cm) and (2) 2½" × 80½" (6.5 cm × 204.5 cm) for outside red borders; subcut (2) 2½" × 72½" (6.5 cm × 184 cm) and (2) 2½" × 76½" (6.5 cm × 194.5 cm) for inside red borders

NOTE: *Use the balance of the red fabric for the "pre-fused" fabric. Lightly label the back of each part and separate the parts by block.*

From "pre-fused" red fabric, cut:

☐ (9) 12½" (31.5cm) × WOF strips; subcut 18 part A for Snowflake blocks

From remaining fabric, cut:

☐ 72 part C for Cactus Flower blocks

☐ 72 part B for Cactus Flower blocks

☐ 18 part A for Cactus Flower blocks

FIGURE 1

FIGURE 2

VARIATIONS

You can use any combination of 12" (30.5 cm) blocks to create this intriguing design, such as the Wild Goose Chase and Unnamed blocks (VARIATION 1) or the Mirror Image and Paper Cut Appliqué blocks (VARIATION 2).

VARIATION 1

VARIATION 2

FIGURE 3

FIGURE 4

FIGURE 5

FIGURE 6

BLOCK ASSEMBLY

1. Following the instructions in chapter 2, make 18 Cactus Flower blocks (FIGURE 1) and 18 Snowflake blocks (FIGURE 2). Trim the blocks to 12½" (31.5 cm) square.

ROW ASSEMBLY

2. To make row set 1, sew 3 Cactus Flower and 3 Snowflake blocks together starting with a Cactus Flower and alternating blocks as shown (FIGURE 3). Press the seams open. Make 3 rows.

3. To make row set 2, sew 3 Snowflake blocks and 3 Cactus Flower blocks together starting with a Snowflake block and alternating blocks as shown (FIGURE 4). Press the seams open. Make 3 rows.

QUILT TOP ASSEMBLY

Refer to FIGURE 5 for steps 4–7.

4. Starting with row set 1, sew the row sets together alternating rows until all 6 rows are sewn together. Press the seams open.

5. Sew (1) 2½" × 72½" (6.5 cm × 184 cm) red inside border strip to the top and 1 to the bottom of the center panel. Then sew (1) 2½" × 76½" (6.5 cm × 194.5 cm) red inside border strip to each side. Press the seams open.

6. Sew (1) 2½" × 76½" (6.5 cm × 194.5 cm) white border strip to the top and 1 to the bottom of the center panel. Then sew (1) 2½" × 80½" (6.5 cm × 204.5 cm) white border strip to each side. Press the seams open.

7. Sew (1) 2½" × 80½" (6.5 cm × 204.5 cm) red border strip to the top and 1 to the bottom of the quilt. Then sew (1) 2½" × 84½" (6.5 cm × 214.5 cm) red border strip to each side (FIGURE 6). Press the seams open.

FINISHING THE QUILT

8. Divide backing into (3) 92" (233 cm) × WOF. Remove the selvedges and sew the panels together. Press seams open.

9. Layer the backing (right-side down), batting, and quilt top (right-side up); baste. Quilt as desired.

10. Join the 2¼" (5.5 cm) binding strips into one continuous piece for straight-grain French-fold binding (see French-Fold Binding in chapter 1). Add the binding to the quilt.

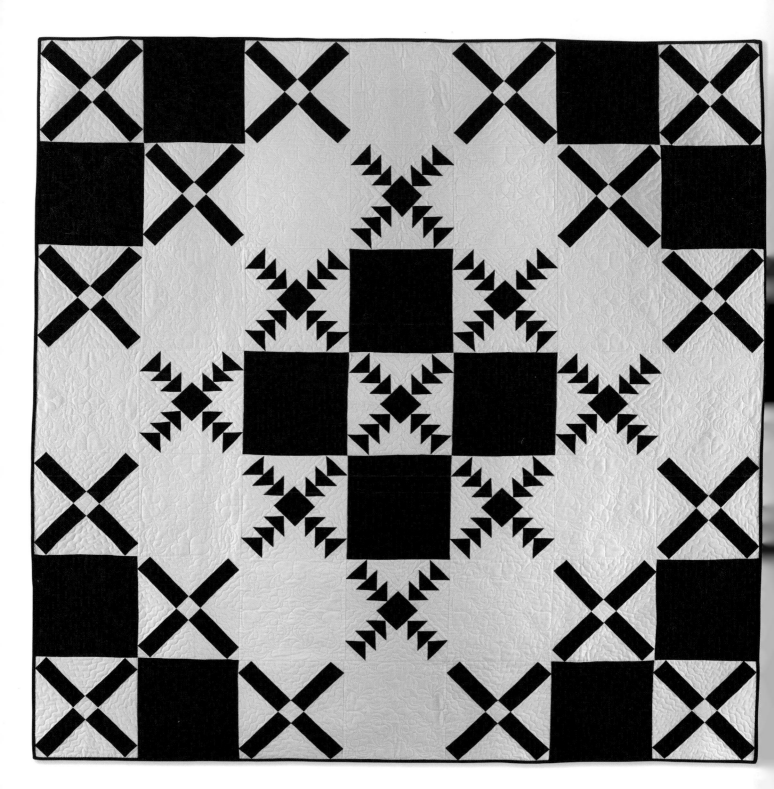

X MARKS THE SPOT QUILT

PIECED BY Linda Pumphrey. MACHINE-QUILTED BY Karen Kielmeyer.

FINISHED SIZE: 84"
(213.5 cm) square

MATERIALS

Yardages are based on 40–42"
(101.6–106.7 cm) wide fabric.

☐ White fabric, 5¼ yards (4.8 m)
☐ Red fabric, 2¾ yards (2.5 m)
☐ Backing fabric, 7¾ yards (7.1 m)
☐ Binding fabric, ¾ yard (0.7 m)
☐ Thread for piecing
☐ Queen-size quilt batting

According to the *Oxford Dictionary*, the expression "X marks the spot" dates back to the early 1800s. In pirate lore, the phrase is used to indicate where buried treasure might lie. Hopefully the quilt you make will be your treasure.

CUTTING INSTRUCTIONS

From white fabric, cut:

☐ (4) 12½" (31.5 cm) × WOF (width-of-fabric) strips; subcut into (12) 12½" (31.5 cm) squares

☐ (3) 2⅝" (6.5 cm) × WOF strips; subcut into (60) 2⅝" (6.5 cm) squares, then cut each square in half diagonally to make 120 half-squares for Flying Geese unit backgrounds

☐ (1) 3¼" (7.5 cm) × WOF strips; subcut into (10) 3" (7.5 cm) squares, then cut each square in half diagonally to make 20 half-squares for Flying Geese Corner units

☐ (4) 2¼" (5.5 cm) × WOF strips; subcut into (40) 2¼" (5.5 cm) squares, then cut the squares in half diagonally to make 80 half-square triangles for Crossroads block corner triangles

☐ (2) 2½" (6.5 cm) × WOF strips; subcut into (20) 2½" (6.5 cm) squares for Crossroads block center squares

☐ (7) 10½" (26.5 cm) × WOF strips; subcut into (20) 10½" (26.5 cm) squares, then cut squares in half diagonally twice to make 80 quarter-square triangles for Crossroads block side triangles

☐ (2) 8⅜" (21.5 cm) strips; subcut into (5) 8⅜" (21.5 cm) squares; subcut each square in half diagonally twice to make 20 quarter-square triangles for Flying Geese side triangles

From red fabric, cut:

☐ (4) 12½" (31.5 cm) × WOF strips; subcut into (12) 12½" (31.5 cm) squares

☐ (3) 3" (7.5 cm) × WOF strips; subcut into (30) 3" (7.5 cm) squares, then cut each square in half diagonally to make 60 half-square triangles to form Flying Geese units

☐ (8) 2½" (6.5 cm) × WOF strips; subcut into (80) 2½" × 7" (6.5 cm × 18 cm) rectangles for Crossroads blocks

☐ (1) 3⅞" (10 cm) × WOF strip; subcut into (5) 3⅞" (10 cm) squares for Wild Goose Chase center blocks

☐ (10) 2¼" (5.5 cm) × WOF strips for the binding

BLOCK ASSEMBLY

1. Following the instructions in chapter 2, make 5 Wild Goose Chase blocks (FIGURE 1) and 20 Crossroads blocks (FIGURE 2).

VARIATIONS

You can use any combination of 12" (30.5 cm) blocks in this eye-catching design, such as Four-Leaf Clover and Nine Patch with Leaves blocks (VARIATION 1) or the Cactus Flower and Lobster blocks (VARIATION 2).

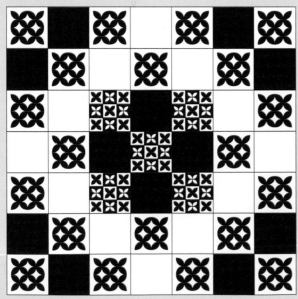

VARIATION 1

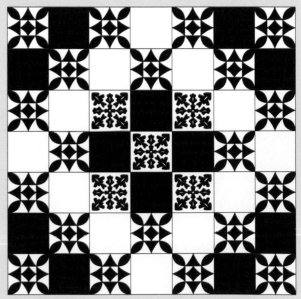

VARIATION 2

FIGURE 1   FIGURE 2

Rows 1 and 7

Rows 2 and 6

Rows 3 and 5

Row 4

FIGURE 3

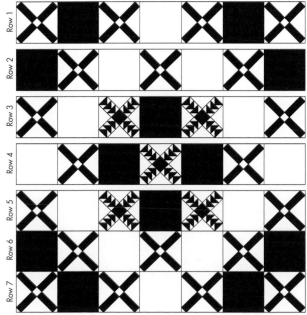

FIGURE 4

QUILT ASSEMBLY

2. Referring to FIGURE 3, sew the blocks together in rows as follows:

▸ **ROWS 1 AND 7:** Sew together in this order 1 Crossroads block, 1 red square, 1 Crossroads block, 1 white square, 1 Crossroads block, 1 red square, and 1 Crossroads block. Press seams open.

▸ **ROWS 2 AND 6:** Sew together in this order 1 red square, 1 Crossroads block, 1 white square, 1 Crossroads block, 1 white square, 1 Crossroads block, and 1 red square. Press seams open.

▸ **ROWS 3 AND 5:** Sew together in this order 1 Crossroads block, 1 white square, 1 Wild Goose Chase block, 1 red square, 1 Wild Goose Chase block, 1 white square, and 1 Crossroads block. Press seams open.

▸ **ROW 4:** Sew together in this order 1 white square, 1 Crossroads block, 1 red square, 1 Wild Goose Chase block, 1 red block, 1 Crossroads block, and 1 white square. Press seams open.

3. Sew the rows together (FIGURE 4). Press the seams open.

FINISHING THE QUILT

4. Divide the backing into (3) 92" (233.5 cm) × WOF lengths. Remove the selvedges and sew panels together. Press seams open.

5. Layer the backing (right-side down), batting, and quilt top (right-side up); baste. Quilt as desired.

6. Join the 2¼" (5.5 cm) binding strips into one continuous piece for straight-grain French-fold binding (see French-Fold Binding in chapter 1). Add the binding to the quilt.

INDEX

RESOURCES

MOUNTAIN MIST BATTING AND FILLER PRODUCTS:
mountainmistcrafts.com

PAPER-BACKED FUSIBLE WEB: warmcompany.com

QUILTING FABRIC: modafabrics.com

QUILTING THREAD: aurifil.com

INTERNATIONAL QUILT STUDY CENTER & MUSEUM: quiltstudy.org

AMERICAN QUILT STUDY GROUP:
americanquiltstudygroup.org

QUILT ALLIANCE: quiltalliance.org

SUGGESTED READING

Mountain Mist Historical Quilts: 14 Mid-Century Quilts Made New, by Linda Pumphrey; Fons & Porter, 2016

America's Glorious Quilts, edited by Dennis Duke and Deborah Harding; Beaux Arts Editions, 1987

Quilting the New Classics: 20 Inspired Quilt Projects, Traditional to Modern Designs, by Michele Muska; Sixth & Spring Books, 2014

The American Quilt: A History of Cloth and Comfort 1750–1950, by Roderick Kiracofe and Mary Elizabeth Johnson; Potter Style, 1993

Quilts in America, by Patsy and Myron Orlofsky; Abbeville Press, 1992

ACKNOWLEDGMENTS

Several individuals joined me again as I started the journey of writing a second book. My books do not happen without help and support during the process. In fact, they would be hard to create if I did not have a wonderful team behind the scenes.

Thank you to my mom and sister, who each made a quilt in the book. Your quilts are wonderful additions to this book. Thank you to Karen Keilmeyer, who partnered with me again and took all the quilt tops and made them into finished quilts with wonderful unique quilting artistry. Thank you to April Wickett, whose illustrations make the written words come to life and give each project a visual road map to the instructions. To my content editor Jodi Butler, you are a dream to work with and so patient. Thanks for taking my written words and making them sound professional. Thank you to Deborah Roberts, whose knowledge of Turkey Red helps me understand why historically red and white has been a favorite combination to quilters for centuries.

Most importantly, thank you to the International Quilt Study Center & Museum and their wonderful staff for preserving the quilts that are the inspiration for the forty blocks in this book. The museum's mission is to "uncover the world through the cultural and artistic significance of quilts, and to research, acquire, and exhibit in all their forms and expressions." Portions of the proceeds for the sales of this book will be donated to the International Quilt Study Center & Museum at Quilt House to benefit that mission. Located on the campus of the University of Nebraska-Lincoln, the IQSCM is a must-see destination for all quilt enthusiasts, quiltmakers, and quilt historians. The accessible collection of quilts, outstanding exhibits, and wonderful staff make any visit exciting.

METRIC CONVERSION CHART

TO CONVERT	TO	MULTIPLY BY
Inches	Centimeters	2.54
Centimeters	Inches	0.4
Feet	Centimeters	30.5
Centimeters	Feet	0.03
Yards	Meters	0.9
Meters	Yards	1.1

VIEWING CONTENTS ON CD

Although it is recommended that you use Adobe Acrobat Reader 9 to view the disk content, your computer may be set up to open PDF files in a different application by default. If your computer does not have an application to view PDF files, you can get the latest version of the free Adobe Acrobat Reader from the Adobe website: http://get.adobe.com/reader/.

Simply copy this URL into your browser's address bar.

ABOUT THE AUTHOR

Linda Pumphrey is an award-winning quilter, designer, and quilt historian, who has a wonderful career in the quilting industry. According to Linda, quilts are much like her career—full of color with different patterns and made of layers. Quilting has been a family passion for at least five generations. She is known for her hand-quilting, for which she has won many awards. Linda serves on several international and national boards, including that of the International Quilt Association, International Quilt Study Center & Museum, and Quilts Inc. Advisory Council. For twenty years, Linda was the National and International Sales Manager for Mountain Mist, the inventor of filler products and quilt battings. While at Mountain Mist, Linda acted as curator of the Historical Mountain Mist Corporate Quilt Collection and was instrumental in bringing the collection to the International Quilt Study Center & Museum at the University of Nebraska-Lincoln. She has just rejoined Fibrix, LLC, the maker of Mountain Mist, as Senior Account Executive for the craft and equine markets.

DEDICATION

This book is dedicated to all the friends I have made through quilting. You keep me inspired, laughing, and my feet on the ground. Also to my mom and sister, who were excited to make a quilt for this book.

WHAT WILL YOU MAKE NEXT?

MOUNTAIN MIST HISTORICAL QUILTS

14 Mid-Century Quilts Made New
BY LINDA PUMPHREY

Traditional designs get
a modern makeover!
This beautifully curated
collection showcases 14
quilts from the celebrated
Mountain Mist Series.

ISBN: 9781440245596 • $24.99

MODERN MACHINE QUILTING

Make A Perfectly Finished Quilt
on Your Home Machine
BY CATHERINE REDFORD

Clean lines, bold colors,
contemporary designs—quilting
has gone modern! And this
book is the ultimate guide for
creating modern quilts on a
standard sewing machine.

ISBN: 9781440246319 • $24.99

WEEKEND QUILTING

Quilt and Unwind with Simple
Designs to Sew in No Time
BY JEMIMA FLENDT

Finding time to quilt doesn't
have to be a luxury or a long-
term commitment. Written for
quilters of all skill levels, this
book features stylish quilts,
cushions, and runners you can
make in a few days or less.

ISBN: 9781440246616 • PRICE: $24.99